THE EFFICIENCY EDGE

Transforming Business Operations for Future Success

MANICKAVASAGAM PALANIANDY

*This book is a tribute to the many people who have shaped
my 27-year journey as a transformation expert.*

*To my mentors and clients, your wisdom and support have been my
guiding light, enriching my path both personally and professionally.*

*To my dedicated coachees and mentees, your humility, dedication, and
unwavering determination inspire me every day. "The Efficiency Edge:
Transforming Business Operations for Future Success" is devoted to
celebrating your triumphs and our shared pursuit of excellence.*

Acknowledgments

Crafting "The Efficiency Edge: Transforming Business Operations for Future Success" has been a profound journey, spanning over two decades of experiences, research, and meaningful collaborations. This book reflects the contributions and support of many remarkable individuals, and for this, I am deeply grateful.

My deepest gratitude is reserved for my wife, Naliney, and our son, Sarnesh. You both have created a nurturing space that allowed my ideas to flourish at all hours, supporting me unwaveringly through every phase of this project. This book stands on the foundation of your love and support.

To my extended family—parents, in-laws, and relatives—your enduring love fortifies me daily, influencing who I am at my core.

I am profoundly thankful to trailblazing leaders like Edwin Nevis, Dato' Arif Siddiqui, Michael Van Noort, Dominic Mascrinas, Sonia Wedrychowicz, Mike Burnett, Martheswaran S., and CY Shong. Your exemplary leadership has shaped my professional journey and lit the path I walk today.

My instructors Karthik Siva, Joel Bauer, and Tony Robbins, along with my spiritual guides and cherished friends, your wisdom has been instrumental in shaping this narrative. To those I've mentored, your growth and insights have added invaluable layers to my understanding and this book.

To my team at Lean Partner, your dedication and excellence, even amidst our demanding schedules, have not gone unnoticed. I cherish your commitment and support deeply.

A special thank you goes to the unsung heroes of this project—the publisher, editor, artwork designer, proofreader, photographer, testimonial contributors, website designer, and everyone spreading the word. Your collective efforts have brought this book to life.

With all my gratitude,

Manickavasagam

Contents

– 1 –

The Foundation of Efficiency in a Transforming World

"Efficiency is doing better what is already being done."

Peter Drucker's words have profoundly shaped my understanding of what lies at the heart of operational excellence. Throughout my years in the field, I've come to realise that at the core of operational excellence is, indeed, operational efficiency—a dynamic force that drives businesses toward success.

Let's start with the crucial step of peeling back the layers of operational efficiency. Understanding this concept is foundational as a practical approach to achieving competitive advantage, sustainability, and customer satisfaction in our fast-paced and complex business environment.

Imagine your business as a high-performance engine. Operational efficiency is the fine-tuning that ensures every part of that engine runs smoothly, with as little waste as possible and the best output achievable. According to Pipefy, this efficiency directly shapes your ability to meet strategic goals, influencing everything from expense projections to revenue growth. Consider this: if your company earns $200,000 in total revenue with $100,000 in operational expenses, your operational efficiency ratio stands at 0.5. This means you're spending half of every dollar earned on running operations.

The roots of operational efficiency trace back to the principles of scientific management developed by Frederick Taylor in the early 20th century. Taylor's work, which focused on scientifically analyzing workflows and labor productivity, laid the groundwork for what we now consider modern operational efficiency. This historical perspective highlights the importance of measuring and optimizing the input-output ratio in business operations.

Further developments were significantly shaped by the lean manufacturing techniques pioneered by Toyota in the mid-20th century, which emphasized waste reduction and continuous improvement, known as Kaizen. Additionally, the Total Quality Management (TQM) movement that emerged post-World War II focused on enhancing product quality and operational processes, further refining our understanding of operational efficiency.

In the latter part of the 20th century and into the 21st, advancements in technology and the globalization of markets have required a more nuanced approach to operational efficiency. Businesses have had to adapt to rapid changes, integrate new technologies, and optimize their operations for cost reduction, agility, quality, and sustainability.

Today, operational efficiency is all about finding smarter ways to run a business. It's about doing more with less - using resources wisely, cutting costs without cutting corners, ensuring quality doesn't slip, and keeping customers happy. It's an ongoing journey of checking in on how things are done, figuring out what could be better, and then making those changes to work smarter, not harder.

The term "operational efficiency" is being redefined and reimagined right before our eyes in the shifting global economy. The driving force behind this change? None other than the COVID-19 pandemic—a global event that has profoundly impacted the way we understand and approach the efficiency of our operations.

The Impact of Global Changes on Operations

The pandemic has forced organizations across various sectors to radically rethink their operational strategies. Beyond staying float, it was about pivoting quickly to maintain productivity, ensure sustainability, and adapt swiftly to new market conditions. Let's delve into how these shifts are reshaping our approach to business operations.

One of the most significant shifts has been the *accelerated pace of digital transformation.* As the world went into lockdown, businesses scrambled to facilitate remote work, enhance digital customer interactions, and improve operational agility. According to the International Monetary Fund (IMF), digitalization in advanced economies jumped by an average of 6 percentage points during the pandemic. This marked a permanent shift towards more digitally-enabled operations that are here to stay.

The changes brought by the pandemic extended into the very soul of workplace environments. A study published in BMC Public Health highlighted a notable *decline in work efficiency and an increase in employee stress* post-lockdown. This new challenge demands that we both reconsider our operational strategies and how we support our workforce. Ensuring worker productivity and well-being has become a pivotal aspect of operational efficiency.

Perhaps nowhere were the impacts of the pandemic felt more acutely than in the domain of supply chains. With *severe supply chain disruptions* that seemed to happen overnight, companies were compelled to reevaluate their operational strategies to enhance resilience and adaptability. According to research, a staggering 92% of companies continued their technology investments during the pandemic, focusing heavily on digital supply chains to navigate these disruptive forces. Today, making supply chains more resilient, collaborative, and networked with real-time visibility and dynamic SKU rationalization is a necessity.

The pandemic truly transformed entire paradigms of operational tactics. Research reports that the approach to vaccine development—a process historically marred by delays and inefficiencies—has been revolutionized, underscoring *the critical importance of agility and speed* in today's business operations. This transformation is reflective of a broader shift across industries where companies must rethink their approaches, focusing on digital operations and advanced analytics to effectively respond to rising costs and rapidly changing market demands.

Exploring how the pandemic has affected operational efficiency brings us to a crucial turning point: **the swift rise of technology**, especially Artificial Intelligence (AI). This is about a whole new way of doing things. I want to dive into how AI is becoming essential for keeping operations efficient and how it's changing the game for businesses everywhere.

The advent of AI in business operations marks a fundamental shift in how we approach efficiency. AI's role is diverse and impactful, ranging from automating mundane tasks to reshaping strategic decision-making frameworks. By automating routine and repetitive tasks, AI has liberated human workers to focus on more complex and value-driven activities. This strategic reallocation is about enhancing the quality of work and fostering innovation within teams.

Consider AI-powered bots and software that manage data entry, invoice processing, and appointment scheduling. These tools streamline workflows and drastically reduce the chances of human error, leading to faster and more reliable processes.

It is estimated that AI could automate 45% of tasks currently performed by humans, particularly those repetitive in nature. This shift allows employees to engage in higher-value tasks—those requiring creativity, problem-solving, and personal interaction.

AI's capability extends beyond task automation into predictive analytics. This feature of AI enhances decision-making processes by enabling businesses to forecast market changes and understand customer needs with unprecedented accuracy. Efficient inventory management, demand forecasting, and maintenance scheduling are now performed with a level of precision that was previously unattainable.

For instance, BMW employs AI for predictive maintenance on their production lines. This application of AI anticipates when equipment maintenance is needed and significantly reduces downtime and maintenance costs. Companies implementing AI for predictive maintenance report up to 50% reduction in equipment downtime and increases in production by as much as 20%.

AI has also revolutionized supply chain management by providing real-time visibility and enhancing the dynamic rationalization of stock-keeping units (SKUs). These advancements lead to optimized logistics costs, better inventory levels, and improved service standards, transforming the way supply chains operate.

Despite AI's profound benefits, its integration into operational processes is not without challenges. High initial investment costs, the necessity for skilled personnel, concerns about potential job displacement, and ethical considerations around data privacy and decision-making transparency are significant hurdles.

Integrating AI into your operations demands a strategic vision and a commitment to developing the necessary skills within your organization. Addressing ethical and practical challenges head-on is crucial for leveraging AI's full potential.

AI is indeed a game-changer in the pursuit of operational efficiency. As businesses, we must be willing to rethink our processes and embrace the possibilities that AI offers. By automating tasks, enhancing decision-making, and optimizing supply chains, AI provides a substantial opportunity to improve the efficiency and the intelligence of our operations.

Operational Efficiency as a Strategic Imperative

Having explored the transformative impact of the pandemic and the advent of AI on our operational domain, it's crucial to dig deeper into how operational efficiency is a cornerstone of strategic business planning. This aspect of business strategy is particularly vital in scenarios where efficiency gains directly contribute to bolstering business resilience. So, let's unpack the essentials of operational efficiency and how it acts as a lifeline during times of uncertainty.

As we have seen, operational efficiency is fundamentally about doing more with less—optimizing processes, resources, and systems to achieve the best possible outcomes without unnecessary expenditure of time and effort. This efficiency is about enabling your business to adapt quickly and effectively to disruptions and changing market conditions.

Integrating operational efficiency into strategic planning requires a systematic approach. It's about dissecting every process, every resource allocation, and system to ensure they are optimized. This meticulous approach is crucial in scenarios where businesses face disruptions that could potentially derail operations.

At its core, *operational efficiency enhances business resilience*. It provides a framework for businesses to continue operating under adverse conditions by ensuring that resources are used judiciously, processes are streamlined, and outcomes are maximized. This kind of efficiency becomes your first line of defense against the unexpected, preparing your organization to thrive.

In today's fast-paced market, *adaptability is key*. Operational efficiency empowers businesses to pivot quickly in response to market conditions. Whether it's a supply chain disruption, a sudden shift in consumer behavior, or a global economic downturn, an operationally efficient business can adjust its strategies swiftly and effectively.

As we progress through this book, we will delve deeper into these topics, providing a comprehensive exploration of operational efficiency. But here, let us touch on an overview, bracing ourselves for the detailed discussions that will follow.

Operational efficiency is strategic imperative for embedding resilience, adaptability, and foresight into every facet of your business operations. Efficient operations help identify potential risks and manage them before they escalate into more significant issues. Efficiency leads to more robust business continuity planning, ensuring that your business can operate under various scenarios without significant disruptions.

By optimizing resource use, operational efficiency ensures that every asset, every piece of technology, and every human resource is utilized to its fullest potential, contributing to overall business sustainability.

Operational efficiency transcends mere buzzword status to become the cornerstone of strategic business planning today. It's about crafting a business that tackles current challenges head-on and possesses the agility to navigate future uncertainties. Remember, as we advance, operational efficiency stands as your strategic ally in forging a resilient, adaptable, and supremely successful enterprise.

As we delve into the strategic aspects of business planning, operational efficiency emerges as a key driver, especially when expanding your business's horizons. Whether you're considering entering new markets or planning to scale up operations, the metrics of operational efficiency guide these crucial decisions, offering a clear roadmap for growth and adaptation.

Understanding and utilizing operational efficiency metrics can make the difference between successful market entry and costly missteps. Metrics such as market growth rate, customer acquisition cost (CAC), and return on investment (ROI) are essential tools for assessing new markets. A high market growth rate suggests a promising opportunity for high returns. Conversely, a lower CAC points to a cost-effective pathway to capturing new customer bases.

For example, a company looks to expand into Southeast Asia, metrics like Average Revenue Per User (ARPU) and market penetration rates can pinpoint where the financial potential lies, guiding strategic decisions on where to focus expansion efforts.

Operational efficiency metrics also dictate the **best way to allocate resources**—be it financial, human, or technological—when entering new territories. Metrics like operational cost ratios and efficiency rates can show how best to use resources to maximize output and minimize waste.Consider an instance here: based on projected ROI, a business may increase its marketing spend or seek local partnerships to maximize entry into a new market.

Efficiency metrics are invaluable for **identifying risks associated with entering new markets**. Analyzing metrics like lead conversion ratios and customer churn rates helps understand market dynamics and customer behaviors, vital for tailoring strategies to local conditions.

A tech company closely monitors early customer feedback and engagement metrics after launching a product in a new market, allowing them to quickly adapt their strategy in response to customer needs and preferences.

Scaling operations requires *a meticulous balance between growth and maintaining quality,* making operational efficiency metrics crucial. As businesses expand, it becomes essential to identify and address inefficiencies that could impede growth. Metrics like production volume, defect rates, and throughput times are valuable for highlighting potential bottlenecks. For instance, a manufacturing company might consider automation technologies to maintain quality as output increases, using production efficiency metrics to guide investment decisions.

Efficient capacity planning is another cornerstone of successful scaling, reliant on metrics such as capacity utilization and demand forecasting. These metrics help ensure that the scaling of the business is in step with actual and projected demands, thus avoiding unnecessary expenditures or experiencing shortages. For example, an e-commerce company might strategically plan inventory and logistics capacity for upcoming peak periods by analyzing past sales data alongside current demand forecasts. This approach allows the company to optimize resources and ensure readiness for increased demand, supporting sustainable growth.

Operational efficiency metrics do far more than just track performance; they *empower businesses to make strategic decisions* that propel growth while managing risks. These metrics help businesses plan their expansions thoughtfully and ensure that they remain competitive and sustainable in the long run.

Building on our discussion about strategic planning and operational efficiency, let's turn our attention to a crucial aspect that directly impacts your bottom line: *customer satisfaction.* With expectations for customer service reaching new heights every year—54% of customers expect more than they did just one year ago, according to a Microsoft survey—the role of operational efficiency in fulfilling these expectations cannot be overstated.

In today's fast-paced market, the speed with which you deliver can set you apart. Operational efficiency streamlines your processes, cutting down the time it takes to get your products or services into the hands of customers. A survey from digital consultancy Avionos found that fast shipping is a key component of a positive retail experience. This connection between operational speed and customer satisfaction is clear: faster service delivery often exceeds customer expectations, enhancing their overall experience.

But speed does not compromise quality. Efficient operations ensure that the quality of products and services is consistently high. This involves fine-tuning production processes, conducting rigorous quality checks, and engaging in continuous improvement practices. By maintaining a high standard of quality, you ensure that customer satisfaction remains high and product returns remain low.

Efficiency also plays a pivotal role in customer service operations. With the right technology and well-defined processes in place, businesses can respond to customer inquiries and resolve issues more quickly and effectively. Efficient customer service operations ensure that every customer interaction is handled swiftly and satisfactorily, leaving a lasting positive impression.

Another benefit of operational efficiency is *effective cost management*, which can translate into competitive pricing or higher value offerings for customers. By keeping operational costs in check, you can offer your products or services at competitive prices, enhancing customer satisfaction and strengthening your market position without sacrificing profit margins.

Today's market demands *personalization*, and operational efficiency enables businesses to offer just that. Efficient data management and processing allow for tailored marketing, product customization, and personalized service, meeting individual customer needs and preferences with precision.

Increasingly, customers care about the environmental impact of their purchases. Operational efficiency leads to more *sustainable practices*, such as reducing waste and optimizing resource use. This satisfies environmentally conscious consumers and contributes to a stronger, more responsible brand image.

These crucial insights point us towards understanding operational efficiency as a robust framework that enhances every touchpoint of the customer experience—from the speed of service delivery and maintaining high-quality standards to responsive customer service and sustainable practices. By focusing on operational efficiency, businesses can ensure they exceed customer expectations, fostering loyalty and driving long-term success.

As we wrap up our discussion on operational efficiency, it's clear how vital this concept is for thriving in today's fast-paced business environment. Embracing operational efficiency transforms businesses into resilient, agile entities ready to face tomorrow's challenges.

Operational efficiency does more than enhance the bottom line; it embeds a culture of excellence and continuous improvement. It prepares businesses to adapt swiftly and align resources efficiently, ensuring they excel, regardless of market conditions.

Moving forward, consider operational efficiency as an ongoing journey that shapes every aspect of your business. Strive to set standards that inspire and lead, forging a legacy of efficiency that propels your business into the future.

– 2 –

Assessing Your Operational Health

"Evaluate your current state to build a future of robust performance'

In the journey toward operational efficiency and the path to excellence, let's take a moment to reflect.

Where do we steer our path after understanding the fundamentals of operational efficiency? You might be considering a slew of strategic innovations or cutting-edge technologies; yet, there's a fundamental aspect that demands your attention first and foremost—operational health. "The greatest wealth is health," declared the ancient poet Virgil. This timeless adage rings especially true in the business world. Just as our personal well-being underpins our daily achievements, the health of an organization's operations is crucial for its sustained success and competitive edge.

Operational health is the bedrock of your business's vitality. It encompasses the critical elements of efficiency, effectiveness, and adaptability—each playing a unique role in how your organization performs and thrives. These elements, while universal in their importance, manifest differently across various industries, from manufacturing to services to technology.

Understanding Operational Health

Building on our discussions from Chapter 1, let's zero in on the first critical element of operational health: **efficiency.** This concept isn't new to us; as we've explored previously, efficiency is the engine driving your business toward reduced costs and maximized productivity. Now, let's delve deeper into how this component shapes your operational health across various industries.

In the world of manufacturing, efficiency is paramount -it's all about doing things better, faster, and smarter. The goal is to make more while wasting less. That's where the magic of Lean Manufacturing and Six Sigma comes in, cutting down the clutter and sharpening quality, all while keeping costs in check. Then, enter the game changers: automation and robotics. They've taken production lines to a whole new level, cranking up precision and pace, and dialing down the need for hands-on work. This shift fosters efficiency by freeing up people to focus on the big picture, making the whole operation run smoother and smarter.

For service-oriented businesses, operational efficiency takes a slightly different form. Here, it revolves around optimizing service delivery to ensure customer satisfaction. This includes reducing wait times, using technology to streamline customer service processes, and enhancing staff training. Software tools that manage customer relationships and service delivery play a crucial role, allowing businesses to respond quicker and more effectively to customer needs, thereby boosting loyalty and retention.

In the technology sector, efficiency is closely linked to the speed and agility of software development and infrastructure management. Adopting Agile methodologies and DevOps practices helps companies accelerate development cycles, improve collaboration across functional teams, and ensure that technological solutions are deployed efficiently and effectively. This speeds up innovation and enhances the ability to respond to market changes swiftly, maintaining a competitive edge.

Unlocking and boosting efficiency transcends smoothing out operations—it's about building a solid base for your operational health to ensure sustainable growth and enduring success. Whether you're crafting products, rolling out services, or innovating tech solutions, think of operational efficiency as your strategic sidekick, making sure every piece of your business puzzle fits perfectly and performs at its peak.

After delving into the crucial role of efficiency in operational health, let's shift our focus to another essential element: **effectiveness**. Effectiveness measures how well your organization achieves its predefined objectives and satisfies customer needs. Whether you're crafting products, delivering services, or developing cutting-edge technologies, effectiveness is about meeting and often exceeding those expectations that define your business's success.

In manufacturing, effectiveness is synonymous with product quality and compliance with industry standards. The primary aim here is to produce excellently—creating reliable products that fulfill customer expectations and adhere to strict regulatory requirements.

Robust quality control systems are non-negotiable in manufacturing. These systems ensure that every product rolling off your production line is free from defects and complies with safety standards. Adopting standards like ISO 9001 for quality management can dramatically enhance both product quality and operational effectiveness. This commitment to quality doesn't just satisfy regulatory demands—it builds trust with your customers, ensuring they return time and again.

For service-oriented businesses, the effectiveness of your operations is reflected directly in how satisfied your customers are and the quality of service delivery you achieve.

High customer satisfaction is the hallmark of effective service delivery. Tools like the Net Promoter Score (NPS) offer invaluable insights into how well your services resonate with your clients. They help pinpoint areas of excellence and opportunities for improvement, guiding your strategy to consistently meet or exceed customer expectations. Delivering high-quality service means responding to customer inquiries and resolving issues both promptly and accurately.

When we pivot to the tech world, we see that success hinges on innovation, outstanding user experiences, and staying relevant in the market. Tech companies are required to meet today's demands while anticipating and shaping the trends of tomorrow.

Staying ahead in technology requires a relentless focus on research and development. Companies renowned for their innovative edge, like Apple and Google, continuously invest in creating new products and enhancing existing ones. This drive for innovation ensures they remain relevant and competitive.

The tech industry evolves at a breakneck pace, and staying relevant means adapting swiftly to new technologies and shifting consumer preferences. Agile and responsive strategies enable tech companies to develop products that meet emerging needs, ensuring their offerings remain essential to users.

By focusing on these elements of operational health, you create a business that meets today's standards and paves the way for future success.

The next vital aspect of operational health that determines an organization's survival and success in today's rapidly changing business world is **adaptability.** As the legendary basketball coach John Wooden aptly put it, "Failure is not fatal, but failure to change might be." This statement rings especially true in business, where adaptability allows companies to navigate uncertainties and respond proactively to the ever-evolving market conditions, customer preferences, and environmental factors.

In the manufacturing sector, adaptability means the ability to quickly adjust and pivot production processes in response to changes in market demand. This adaptability can take the form of modular production systems that allow for rapid changes in product lines or the implementation of flexible manufacturing practices that can accommodate custom orders without disrupting standard operations. Additionally, the integration of advanced digital technologies enables manufacturers to perform real-time market analysis, further enhancing their ability to react swiftly and effectively to market shifts.

For service industries, adaptability is crucial in how services are offered and delivered. This sector needs to remain flexible to meet changing customer expectations, which might include adopting new service technologies or tailoring services to individual needs. For instance, a financial services firm may introduce remote advisory services to adapt to clients' preferences for digital interaction, or a healthcare provider might offer telehealth options in response to increased demand for remote medical consultations. Adapting service protocols in real-time in response to consumer behavior changes is another critical aspect, ensuring that the service delivery remains relevant and effective.

In the technology sector, adaptability is fundamental for maintaining competitiveness amid rapid technological evolution and shifting market trends. This sector demands a culture that prioritizes continuous learning and an ongoing commitment to research and development. Tech companies must remain agile, ready to pivot strategies or alter product offerings based on real-time feedback and emerging technological advancements.

Remember, adaptability isn't just about survival—it's about thriving. It's about ensuring your business remains relevant, responsive, and ready to meet the future with confidence.

Benchmarks for a Healthy Operation

Having explored the foundational pillars of operational health—efficiency, effectiveness, and adaptability—it's time to focus on how these elements are measured against industry standards. Understanding the benchmarks and key metrics specific to your industry is crucial for gauging the health of your operations and steering them towards optimal performance.

Operational health, while grounded in universal principles, manifests differently across sectors. Each industry has its set of benchmarks and standards that define what optimal operation looks like. Let's delve into some of the key performance indicators (KPIs) and best practices that mark the pulse of operational health across various industries.

Let's start with efficiency metrics.Efficiency across any sector boils down to maximizing outputs while minimizing inputs. Several key metrics universally apply to measure this operational efficiency.

Throughput measures the amount of product or service produced over a given period and is a critical indicator of efficiency. In manufacturing, high throughput rates often signify efficient production lines, indicating the organization's ability to deliver products effectively. Similarly, in the service sector, high throughput might be reflected in the number of customers served or queries resolved within a specific timeframe, highlighting the capability to handle high volumes efficiently.

The utilization rate is another essential metric, evaluating how effectively a company utilizes its resources, such as machinery, workforce, and technology. An optimal utilization rate ensures that resources are fully employed but not overstretched, maintaining a balance that prevents burnout and reduces wear and tear. This careful management helps extend the lifespan of assets and maintains high productivity without compromising the quality of outputs.

Cycle time, which refers to the time required to complete a process from start to finish, is a further measure of operational efficiency. For example, in healthcare, reducing the cycle time for patient processing enhances efficiency and improves patient satisfaction by minimizing wait times. In the retail sector, cycle time may relate to how quickly inventory turns over or the speed at which customer transactions are processed. Shorter cycle times indicate more streamlined and efficient operations, allowing businesses to serve more customers effectively and manage resources more proficiently.

As we delve further into the benchmarks defining operational health, it is crucial to focus on another fundamental aspect: effectiveness. Effectiveness transcends merely executing tasks correctly—it encompasses doing the right actions to achieve goals and meet the expectations of those who rely on your products or services.

Effectiveness within an organization is measured by how well it achieves its objectives and fulfills the needs of its stakeholders, using several key metrics to quantify success. At the core of measuring effectiveness is *customer satisfaction.* High customer satisfaction scores are undeniable indicators that a business is meeting or surpassing customer expectations. These scores provide immediate feedback from customers about their experiences, offering direct insights into the impact of your products or services.

Quality metrics also play a vital role in assessing effectiveness. Metrics such as defect rates, return rates, and adherence to quality standards provide a clear indication of how products or services perform in real-world scenarios. Low defect and return rates are not merely positive signs of product performance; they reflect strong quality management systems. Compliance with established quality standards further underscores the effectiveness of your operations.

Another critical metric is the **Net Promoter Score (NPS)**, which measures customer loyalty and their likelihood to recommend your products or services. A high NPS indicates that customers are not only satisfied but are also enthusiastic advocates of your brand. This score is a direct measure of your operational effectiveness in creating valuable experiences for customers that are compelling enough to encourage recommendations.

Understanding and monitoring these effectiveness metrics allows you to directly connect with what's working and what's not within your operational strategy. They offer tangible, actionable data that can lead to informed decisions about product development, customer service strategies, and overall business tactics.

For instance, if customer satisfaction scores are lagging, it might prompt a review of customer service policies or product quality. Similarly, a dip in NPS might lead to enhanced customer engagement strategies or refinement of your product offerings to better meet customer needs. Each metric serves both as a checkpoint and as a springboard for refinement.

Now that we've explored the concepts of efficiency and effectiveness, let's shift our focus to adaptability, another critical component of operational health. Adaptability is about an organization's ability to thrive amidst changes, reflecting its responsiveness to evolving market conditions, environmental shifts, and changing customer preferences.

One key metric for assessing adaptability is *the time to market*. This metric indicates how quickly a company can move from concept to commercialization, bringing new products or services to consumers. A shorter time to market not only shows an organization's agility but also its capacity to seize new opportunities swiftly. In today's fast-paced market environment, the ability to launch innovations rapidly offers a significant competitive edge.

Changeover time is another crucial adaptability metric. It measures the speed at which an organization can transition from producing one product or service to another. Lower changeover times indicate a more flexible production process, allowing a company to respond quickly to market demands without considerable downtime or loss of productivity.

Lastly, *the rate of innovation* is a strong indicator of an organization's adaptiveness. This metric reflects how frequently a company introduces new products or implements process improvements.A high rate of innovation indicates that an organization is maintaining momentum, adeptly forecasting market trends, and proactively addressing future challenges.

These metrics offer tangible evidence of your organization's capability to adapt and pivot. They provide a clear picture of how prepared your business is to face uncertainties and how effectively it can turn potential disruptions into avenues for growth.

For example, monitoring time to market helps you understand if your product development processes are as streamlined as they should be, or if there are bottlenecks that could hinder your response to a sudden opportunity. Similarly, analyzing changeover times can lead to improvements in your operational processes, making them more flexible and less susceptible to market volatilities.

Understanding and improving these metrics of operational health can transform your organization, making it more responsive and resilient in the face of change.

Adapting SWOT for Operational Insights

After exploring industry benchmarks, it's crucial to turn our attention inward and engage in a thorough self-assessment of our operational processes. A SWOT analysis serves as an effective tool in this endeavor, providing a structured approach to enhance efficiency, effectiveness, and adaptability by identifying strengths, weaknesses, opportunities, and threats within your operations.

Starting with *strengths*, it's important to evaluate the core aspects that underpin your operational health. One critical area is process efficiency, particularly through the lens of automation. Assessing the extent of automation within your operations can reveal much about your efficiency levels. High automation speeds up production or service delivery and significantly reduces the potential for human error. Consider the areas where your processes are automated and identify opportunities where further automation could drive substantial improvements.

Another aspect of operational strength is the integration of lean management practices. How deeply are techniques like Just-In-Time (JIT) or the 5S methodology embedded in your daily operations? The effective implementation of these practices is a testament to operational prowess, as they are designed to minimize waste and optimize workflow, thereby enhancing agility and efficiency.

Moving to quality control, it's essential to measure the consistency and reliability of your output. A low rate of defects or customer complaints directly reflects operational excellence. Ensuring consistent quality in your products or services helps maintain customer satisfaction and loyalty, which are pivotal for long-term success. Additionally, highlight any quality certifications your organization has attained, such as ISO 9001. These certifications represent a commitment to global quality standards and signify your ongoing dedication to operational improvement.

As we assess the operational health of an organization, it is crucial to delve into the expertise and morale of the workforce, which are foundational to any business's success.

Firstly, consider the skill levels across your workforce, particularly in areas central to your operations. High skill levels enhance your operational capabilities and equip your business to effectively tackle complex challenges. This wealth of expertise is a significant asset, creating a solid framework that supports all facets of your operations.

Additionally, employee satisfaction is a vital aspect of your organizational health. High employee satisfaction often leads to enhanced productivity and reduced turnover rates. When employees are content and morale is high, they are more likely to be productive, innovative, and deeply committed to the success of the company. The correlation between employee satisfaction and operational success cannot be overstated, as satisfied employees are crucial drivers of innovation and efficiency.

Understanding these strengths within your workforce is just the beginning. The real challenge—and indeed the opportunity—lies in effectively leveraging these strengths to optimize and expand your operations. Each strength identified acts as a foundational building block for greater operational success, providing a clear path forward for strategic enhancements and sustained growth in the business landscape.

Building on our exploration of strengths, it's important to pivot our attention to areas where our operations might be lacking. ***Recognizing and addressing weaknesses*** is crucial for fortifying operational health. Let's delve into some of the internal challenges that could be hindering your organization's performance and explore strategies to mitigate these issues.

A significant weakness that can affect operations is the age and condition of your equipment. Outdated or malfunctioning equipment can lead to operational delays and escalate maintenance costs, impacting your bottom line. Take a moment to assess the state of your machinery and technology. Consider whether there are tools that frequently require repairs or if outdated technology is slowing your team down.

Financial constraints are another critical area that can limit your ability to make necessary upgrades or expand operational capacities. Reflect on how budget limitations are affecting your operations. It's important to identify areas where insufficient funds are preventing you from achieving optimal efficiency and explore potential solutions or alternative strategies that may require less financial outlay.

Identifying bottlenecks in your production or service delivery processes is also vital. These are the points in your process that cause delays and increase cycle times, directly impacting your ability to meet customer expectations promptly. Determine where these bottlenecks occur within your operations and what causes them. Understanding these can help you devise strategies to alleviate these blockages and enhance flow.

Furthermore, redundant processes that consume resources without adding value represent another common area of weakness. Carefully scrutinize your operations to pinpoint any activities that could be streamlined or eliminated altogether. Assess if there are steps in your process that duplicate efforts or could benefit from automation to reduce waste and improve efficiency.

In the domain of operational health, compliance and risk management are paramount. Ensuring adherence to regulatory compliance is crucial, as non-compliance can lead to significant legal penalties and potentially severe damage to your organization's reputation. It's vital to evaluate how thoroughly your organization follows industry regulations. Investigate the strength of your compliance checks and identify any gaps that might exist in your adherence to these necessary regulations. This careful scrutiny ensures that your operations stay within legal boundaries and uphold the highest standards of corporate governance.

Equally important is the assessment of your risk management practices. Inadequate risk management can leave your organization vulnerable to operational instability and unexpected crises. Reflect on how well-prepared your business is to handle potential risks. Are your risk management protocols comprehensive, up-to-date, and actively maintained? Consider whether these practices are sufficient to cover all areas of your business and whether they're integrated effectively across your operations. Strengthening these areas can significantly fortify your organization's resilience, ensuring that it remains robust in the face of both predictable challenges and unforeseen events.

By understanding where your operations may be falling short, you can begin to implement strategic changes that will enhance your resilience and efficiency. Consider potential improvements or investments that could turn these weaknesses into areas of growth.

As you reflect on these vulnerabilities, think about actionable steps you can take to strengthen these areas.

After examining the weaknesses within our operational framework, it's essential to shift our perspective outward and *identify the opportunities* that can propel us forward. The dynamic business environment offers a wealth of opportunities, often stemming from external innovations and market changes that can significantly enhance our operational capabilities.

Technological advancements present a wealth of opportunities to transform our operations. Emerging technologies like the Internet of Things (IoT), Artificial Intelligence (AI), and blockchain can revolutionize the way we work. Imagine integrating IoT to optimize asset tracking and inventory management, or using AI to automate complex data analyses, improving our decision-making processes. These technologies are practical tools that can boost our efficiency and transparency. Upgrading our automation tools can also streamline operations and reduce our reliance on manual labor, cutting long-term costs and increasing overall efficiency. Think about the areas within our operations where these tools could make a significant impact.

Exploring new markets is another exciting opportunity. Expanding into new geographic or demographic areas can help us grow our customer base and scale our operations. By analyzing market trends and consumer behaviors, we can identify new markets that align with our business goals and capabilities. Strategic partnerships offer additional avenues for growth. Collaborating with businesses whose strengths complement ours can open doors to new markets, shared resources, and enhanced technological capabilities. These partnerships can create synergies that drive innovation and efficiency in ways we might not achieve alone.

Leveraging these opportunities effectively is key to our success. For each opportunity, consider how it might impact our operations and develop strategies to implement changes or adaptations that will maximize these benefits.

Having identified potential opportunities that could elevate our operational capabilities, we must also remain vigilant about the external *threats* that could challenge our progress. Understanding these threats enables us to prepare our operations to respond effectively and maintain stability in the face of adversity.

Competitive pressures pose a significant threat to operational health. The entry of new competitors into the market can intensify these pressures, potentially leading to price wars and reduced profit margins. Monitoring new entrants and considering strategies to differentiate our offerings is crucial to maintaining a competitive edge. Additionally, innovations by competitors can disrupt the market and render existing operational processes obsolete. Staying informed about competitors' moves and considering how to leverage or counteract their innovations with our own strategic initiatives is essential.

Regulatory changes are another critical threat. The regulatory frameworks are continuously evolving, and new regulations can impose significant operational burdens or necessitate costly compliance measures. Keeping abreast of these changes and planning for compliance is essential to avoid legal pitfalls and ensure uninterrupted operations. For industries such as manufacturing, changes in environmental regulations can particularly impact operational processes. Monitoring these regulations is crucial to adapt practices accordingly and avoid potential fines or operational shutdowns.

Economic fluctuations also present substantial threats. Economic downturns or geopolitical tensions can lead to disruptions in the supply chain, affecting the availability and cost of raw materials. Understanding these risks and developing contingency plans can help mitigate the impact on operations. For businesses involved in international trade, fluctuations in currency exchange rates can significantly affect operational costs and profitability. Monitoring these fluctuations and employing risk management strategies such as hedging can help stabilize financial planning.

Recognizing these threats is a proactive step towards enhancing operational resilience. Being prepared to address competitive pressures, regulatory changes, and economic fluctuations will help ensure that our operations remain stable and capable of responding effectively to any challenges that arise.

By focusing on these aspects within the SWOT analysis, you gain a comprehensive understanding of where your operations currently stand and how external factors might influence your future trajectory. These insights empower you to steer your operational strategies toward mitigating risks and leveraging any potential challenges as opportunities for growth and innovation.

Method for Pinpointing Inefficiencies

After conducting a thorough SWOT analysis, it's clear that the next critical step is to delve deeper into specific processes to uncover any inefficiencies that may be hindering your operational health. One effective technique to achieve this is process mining, a powerful tool that utilizes data to paint an accurate picture of how your operations actually unfold.

Process mining stands at the forefront of operational analysis by leveraging event logs from your existing information systems to provide a clear, objective view of your business processes. This method isn't just about identifying what's going wrong—it's about systematically understanding every facet of your operations to foster continual improvement.

At the foundation of process mining is ***automated process discovery***. This involves automatically generating a visual model of your processes using existing data logs. This model presents the reality of your operations, often revealing discrepancies between what is believed to happen and what actually occurs. It's a crucial first step in diagnosing inefficiencies and pinpointing areas where processes do not align with planned models.

Conformance checking follows, where the observed processes (derived from your data logs) are compared against pre-established models or standards. This comparison often highlights deviations that may be undermining your operational efficiency, such as steps that take too long or are skipped entirely. It's particularly vital for ensuring compliance and maintaining rigorous quality control.

Consider a global telecommunications vendor that turned to process mining and uncovered significant inefficiencies within their operations. By automating certain processes and integrating virtual agents and AI, they were able to streamline operations and save nearly $8 million annually. This example underscores the cost-saving potential of process mining and its impact on operational agility.

In the healthcare sector, a provider utilized process mining to examine patient flows through emergency departments. The data revealed critical bottlenecks in patient registration and treatment processes. Armed with this information, they redesigned their workflows, significantly reducing wait times and enhancing the overall quality of care. This improved patient satisfaction and boosted the efficiency of care delivery.

As you consider integrating process mining into your operational analysis toolkit, think about the specific areas in your workflow that could benefit from such deep insights. Which processes seem opaque or unwieldy? Where do errors or delays frequently occur?

Now, reflect on how process mining could transform your operational health. What specific changes could you implement to turn these insights into actionable improvements? Remember, the goal here is not just to find out what is going wrong but to pave the way for what can go right.

Unveiling Inefficiencies with Workflow Analysis

Building on the insights gained from process mining, workflow analysis emerges as another critical tool for enhancing your operational health. This method scrutinizes the flows of work within your organization to pinpoint inefficiencies and identify actionable areas for improvement.

Applicable across various business activities, workflow analysis is instrumental in enhancing both operational efficiency and effectiveness.

Focusing on linear workflows is particularly effective in environments such as assembly lines or administrative procedures where tasks must follow a strict sequence of operations. By examining these linear workflows, you can identify and eliminate unnecessary steps that slow down operations, streamlining processes to enhance efficiency.

In scenarios where workflows span multiple departments or teams, cross-functional workflow analysis becomes essential. This technique is invaluable for uncovering communication barriers and inefficiencies that occur across different parts of your organization. It ensures coherence and coordination across various functional areas, optimizing the overall workflow and boosting collaborative efficiency.

For more complex scenarios involving a mix of sequential and parallel tasks, hybrid workflow analysis is applied. This method examines these intricate workflows to ensure they are optimally designed, balancing the needs of different parts of the workflow and ensuring smooth and efficient integration across all involved processes.

Consider a manufacturing company that applied workflow analysis to their order-to-cash process. By meticulously analyzing each step, they identified redundant tasks and significant bottlenecks that were causing delays. The subsequent streamlining of the process reduced cycle times and enhanced customer satisfaction by delivering orders faster and more reliably.

In the banking sector, a detailed workflow analysis of the loan approval process uncovered several inefficiencies. The bank discovered that multiple manual checks bogged down the procedure. By automating some of these steps and reorganizing the workflow, they significantly cut down the approval time, increasing the efficiency of loan processing and improving customer service.

As you consider these examples and techniques, think about the workflows within your own organization. Where might inefficiencies be hiding? Which processes could benefit from a more streamlined approach? Workflow analysis offers a structured method to uncover these inefficiencies and provides the insights needed to make informed improvements.

Reflect on how you can apply linear, cross-functional, or hybrid workflow analysis to enhance your operational processes. Could simplifying a complicated workflow improve efficiency? Might enhancing communication between departments speed up decision-making?

As we continue, remember that the ultimate goal is to ensure that every part of your operation is as effective, efficient, and adaptable as possible.

Embracing Predictive Analytics in Operational Health

In our journey to enhance operational health, after pinpointing inefficiencies, it's crucial to harness the power of the latest innovations in diagnostic tools, especially in this AI-driven era. Predictive analytics and AI diagnostics are game-changers that offer real-time insights and forecasts, empowering organizations to proactively manage and optimize their operations.

This technology harnesses statistical algorithms and machine learning to predict future outcomes based on historical data. It's a transformative tool that extends beyond simple analysis to anticipate future trends and behaviors, enabling businesses to act rather than react.

Predictive analytics excels in forecasting future customer demands, which allows businesses to finely tune their production schedules, manage inventory levels efficiently, and allocate resources more effectively. This foresight helps in maintaining a balance between supply and demand, ensuring that businesses neither overproduce nor face shortages.

By integrating sensors and IoT devices, predictive analytics can monitor the condition of equipment in real-time. It analyzes this data to predict when maintenance should be carried out, thus preventing unexpected breakdowns and prolonging the machinery's lifespan. This approach reduces downtime and saves costs associated with emergency repairs and replacements.

Another critical application of predictive analytics is in identifying potential operational risks by analyzing patterns and trends that precede disruptions. This insight allows businesses to prepare and implement strategies to mitigate these risks before they manifest into larger issues.

Consider how a leading automotive manufacturer integrates predictive analytics into their operations. By analyzing real-time data from their manufacturing lines, they can anticipate production bottlenecks and dynamically adjust their workflows and resource allocations. This proactive management significantly reduces downtime and enhances overall production efficiency.

Major retailers leverage predictive analytics to refine their supply chain operations. By predicting consumer buying patterns and anticipating peak shopping periods, they manage their inventory with high precision. This optimization reduces excess stock and shortage scenarios, leading to cost savings and boosted customer satisfaction by ensuring products are available when and where they are needed.

Predictive analytics represents a pivotal shift in how businesses approach operational health. It's about moving from a reactive posture to a proactive stance, where decisions are informed by data-driven forecasts that spell out what the future holds.As you reflect on the potential of predictive analytics within your own organization, think about the areas that could benefit most from this advanced foresight.

AI-Driven Diagnostics: Enhancing Operational Insight

Building on the momentum set by predictive analytics, let's explore another revolutionary tool reshaping operational health: AI-driven diagnostics. This advanced application of artificial intelligence, including machine learning and deep learning, delves deeper into your operational data, uncovering inefficiencies and diagnosing issues that often go unnoticed by human analysts.

AI-driven diagnostics harness the power of AI technologies to provide a comprehensive analysis of operational activities, offering insights and actionable intelligence. These tools are designed to detect subtle patterns and anomalies that might escape traditional analysis, providing a deeper understanding of the intricacies of your operations.

AI systems excel in monitoring operational data streams continuously. They provide real-time alerts to managers about anomalies that could signify potential issues, such as unexpected drops in production quality or unusual machine behavior. This immediate feedback allows for swift interventions, potentially averting operational crises before they escalate.

Beyond mere detection, AI-driven diagnostics employ sophisticated algorithms to analyze complex datasets quickly and accurately. They identify the underlying causes of operational issues, enabling businesses to address the root of the problem rather than merely treating the symptoms. This deep-dive analysis ensures that solutions are both effective and enduring.

One of the most transformative applications of AI in diagnostics is its ability to simulate various operational scenarios and predict their outcomes. This capability allows businesses to experiment with different strategies in a virtual environment, choosing those that yield the best outcomes. As a result, operational processes are optimized for peak performance.

Consider a global energy company that employs AI-driven diagnostics to monitor their power generation equipment. The AI system analyzes sensor data to predict failures and recommend preventive maintenance. This proactive approach has led to a significant reduction in unplanned outages, enhancing both operational efficiency and energy production continuity.

Hospitals are increasingly adopting AI diagnostics to optimize various operational processes, such as patient flow and resource allocation. By analyzing trends in patient admissions and identifying bottlenecks in patient care, these systems help improve service delivery and patient outcomes, showcasing the direct impact of AI on operational health.

These tools empower businesses to preemptively tackle challenges, refine processes, and make informed decisions that promote efficiency, reduce costs, and improve overall performance. The examples from the energy and healthcare sectors underline the broad applicability and transformative potential of these technologies across various industries.

As we delve into refining operational processes and addressing inefficiencies, it's crucial to understand that the battle for operational health is ongoing. It doesn't end with implementing solutions; it requires continuous vigilance and adaptation. In this crucial part of our journey, we focus on the significance of ongoing assessments—your dynamic toolset for ensuring that your operations meet standards and evolve with them.

The Critical Role of Ongoing Assessments in Operational Health

Imagine your operations as a living, breathing entity in a constantly changing environment. Just as a navigator must continually check their course and speed against the weather and sea conditions, so must you continually assess and adjust your operational strategies. This continuous cycle of evaluation and improvement is aimed at keeping your operations healthy and making them thrive.

Regular assessments act like a diagnostic tool that continuously scans for inefficiencies or bottlenecks. This ongoing scrutiny allows you to catch and address issues early, often before they can manifest into more significant problems. Think of it as preventive maintenance for your operational processes.

The business landscape is anything but static. Changes in market conditions, technological advancements, and customer preferences are constant. Ongoing assessments provide the agility to adapt quickly to these changes, ensuring that your operations are always aligned with external demands and opportunities.

In today's fast-paced business environment, the ability to continuously improve can set you apart from the competition. Regular assessments help you fine-tune your operations, enhancing efficiency and effectiveness. This commitment to continual improvement can lead to superior product quality, faster service delivery, and more innovative solutions—all of which can significantly boost your competitive edge.

Effective risk management is about foreseeing potential issues and mitigating them before they impact your business. Through ongoing assessments, you can identify emerging risks and trends that might threaten operational stability. This proactive approach safeguards against disruptions and ensures that your business continues to operate smoothly under various circumstances.

As you integrate ongoing assessments into your operational practices, consider them as your eyes and ears in the field. They provide critical insights that inform your decisions, helping you to respond to the present and strategically plan for the future.

After recognizing the importance of ongoing assessments, let's explore how to systematize these into actionable improvements using the *the DMAIC cycle*. Originating from the Six Sigma methodology, this cycle—Define, Measure, Analyze, Improve, and Control—is a strategy for transforming the way we tackle efficiency and quality in our operations.

The journey towards operational excellence begins with the *Define phase*, where the focus is on identifying the specific challenges or opportunities within your operations. This stage demands a thorough understanding of the process in question, its impact on customer satisfaction, and how it aligns with your organizational goals. Crafting a project charter during this stage is crucial; it helps crystallize your problem statement, defines the project scope, and clarifies team roles.

Start by identifying the core issues—whether it's customer dissatisfaction, operational delays, or quality defects. Setting clear objectives is next, ensuring that each goal is framed within the SMART criteria to ensure they are specific, measurable, achievable, relevant, and time-bound. Assembling a project team from various facets of your operations can enrich the problem-solving process with a diversity of insights and potential solutions.

Moving into the *Measure phase*, establishing a baseline is key. This stage provides a clear view of current performance through relevant Key Performance Indicators (KPIs). Selecting the right metrics is crucial; they should directly reflect the performance issues identified. Data collection is the next step, requiring either a review of historical data or the capture of real-time data to create an accurate baseline for comparison. With this data in hand, you can scrutinize performance gaps and prepare for a deeper dive into their causes, setting the stage for effective analysis and subsequent improvements.

The ***Analyze phase*** delves into the 'why'—uncovering the root causes behind identified inefficiencies. This crucial stage involves a detailed analysis of data to unravel the layers of each problem. You can apply analytical tools like the 5 Whys or fishbone diagrams to trace issues back to their origins, employing statistical tools to validate these root causes and assess their impact. The next step is to prioritize these causes, focusing on those that are most critical and addressable, thus setting the stage for targeted improvements.

In the ***Improve phase***, strategic planning transforms into actionable steps. Here, you'll brainstorm potential fixes, developing solutions that are both innovative and practical. Pilot testing these solutions on a small scale allows for the assessment of their effectiveness, enabling necessary fine-tuning before a broader implementation. Once verified, these successful strategies are rolled out, with a strong emphasis on ensuring all team members are fully briefed and on board with the new procedures.

The ***Control phase*** is essential for cementing the improvements made. It involves establishing ongoing monitoring and control mechanisms to sustain the enhancements. Develop detailed control plans that outline how the new processes will be continuously monitored and who will bear the responsibility. All relevant documentation should be updated to reflect the new processes, ensuring consistency and compliance. Regular monitoring of performance against established standards is crucial to maintain continuous compliance and swiftly address any deviations, ensuring the long-term sustainability of operational improvements.

Through the DMAIC cycle, you commit to a path of never-ending improvement, fostering a culture that not only strives for efficiency but thrives on it.

Consider a manufacturing company facing delays in its assembly line. The company employs the DMAIC cycle to address these delays in a structured manner.

Firstly, they define the issue by pinpointing a bottleneck in their assembly line as the primary cause of delays. They establish a clear objective to reduce these delays by reorganizing the workflow and incorporating automated sorting systems.

Next, they measure the existing conditions before making any changes by collecting data on current production speeds and defect rates. This measurement stage is crucial as it establishes a baseline for comparison and provides a clear metric for assessing improvement.

In the analyze phase, the company uses the collected data to scrutinize the processes around the bottleneck. They identify inefficiencies in the workflow and pinpoint areas where automated sorting could expedite production without compromising the quality of the output.

Moving into the improve phase, based on their analysis, the company opts to reorganize the workflow and integrate automated sorting systems. They initiate this process with a pilot project on one assembly line to test the effectiveness of these changes.

Finally, in the control phase, after observing significant improvements in the pilot—marked by faster production speeds and reduced defect rates—the company rolls out these changes across all production lines. They update their standard operating procedures to reflect the new practices and establish ongoing monitoring to ensure the sustained success of these improvements.

This example of the DMAIC cycle illustrates how a methodical, data-driven approach can lead to significant enhancements in operational efficiency. This structured approach clarifies the steps needed for continuous improvement and demonstrates how iterative testing and adaptation can lead to substantial enhancements in operational efficiency.

As we close this discussionon assessing your operational health, consider how the journey toward excellence is a continuous path of discovery and refinement. You've explored the nuances of operational health—understanding its vital components, setting benchmarks, and adapting strategies tailored to your unique challenges. Reflect on the health of your operations as if it were a living, breathing entity within your organization. As you move forward, let the concepts and strategies you've gathered guide your steps. Let each assessment, each cycle of improvement, bring you closer to the pinnacle of operational excellence.

– 3 –

A Foundation for Operational Excellence

*"Operational excellence begins with a solid foundation,
paving the way for success"*

Transitioning from the notion of operational health, let's explore a concept that has profoundly influenced my professional path and understanding of business efficiency—operational excellence.This term, one of the most profound yet complex I've encountered, gradually revealed its importance through years of education and practical experience. Operational excellence isn't just about meeting standards; it's about exceeding them, consistently outperforming the competition by mastering the art of doing things better.

Understanding Operational Excellence

Michael Sony, a noted business writer, succinctly defines operational excellence as "making improvements to attain a competitive advantage." This notion was first developed by Dr. Joseph Juran in the 1970s. Working with Japanese business leaders, Juran laid the groundwork for what would become a pivotal movement in operational management, particularly in manufacturing. His teachings led to the creation of the Shingo Model, a comprehensive framework that encapsulates the essence of operational excellence.

The Shingo Institute, inspired by Dr. Juran's methodologies, has articulated ten principles of Operational Excellence that lay the foundation for a transformative way of thinking, applicable across all facets of an organization. These principles guide a culture that is dynamic and deeply committed to continual improvement.

Central to the Shingo Model is the profound *respect for every individual involved* in the organization, from management to frontline employees, and extending to customers, suppliers, and business partners. This respect is about more than just words; it involves actively involving everyone in improvement processes, empowering them, and fostering their commitment and initiative. When people feel genuinely valued and see their potential to make meaningful contributions, it cultivates a culture where everyone is motivated and engaged.

Leadership within this framework requires *humility*. Operational excellence is fostered by leaders who recognize their limitations and are open to insights from others within the organization. Humble leadership involves actively seeking feedback, listening genuinely, and fostering an environment where team members are encouraged to share innovative ideas and take calculated risks. This approach nurtures a vibrant, adaptable culture crucial for sustained improvement.

The *pursuit of perfection*, although seemingly like chasing a mirage, is essential as it drives continuous boundary pushing and improvement. It's about seeking comprehensive solutions and refining processes to address problems effectively and thoroughly. This relentless pursuit instills a culture where excellence is the norm, not merely a fortuitous outcome.

Operational excellence is also driven by *a commitment to scientific thinking*, which encourages innovation through continuous learning and experimentation. Embracing this mindset means being open to new ideas, taking calculated risks, and valuing the lessons learned from each endeavor. This scientific approach fosters a culture where all team members, including leadership, are empowered to experiment and innovate without fear of failure, supporting a cycle of ongoing improvement and excellence.

When things go awry, it's tempting to point fingers, but the real culprit is often the process, not the people. A flawed process can hamper even the most skilled employees, preventing them from delivering consistent, high-quality results. Rather than hastily assigning blame, it's vital to delve into the process itself to identify where the breakdown occurred. This **shift in focus** fosters a culture of collective responsibility for improvement, encouraging a more supportive and collaborative work environment.

Quality must be assured right from the source, achieved by performing each task correctly with the right tools and understanding from the outset. If undesirable outcomes arise, tracing these issues back to their origins to address the root causes is crucial. Organizing workspaces to highlight potential problems and halting production to correct errors as they are detected can prevent minor issues from escalating into larger, more costly problems.

The heartbeat of any business operation is *delivering maximum value to customers*, ensuring that workflows and processes flow smoothly without interruption, as disruptions can lead to waste and inefficiency. By adopting a 'pull' system that closely aligns production with customer demands, businesses can minimize waste and enhance responsiveness and flexibility, ensuring that nothing is produced without a direct request from the customer.

In any organization, various elements are interconnected, forming a complex system that operates as a whole. *Systemic thinking* involves understanding these connections and using this knowledge to make informed decisions about process improvements. Employees should be encouraged to see beyond the narrow scope of their individual roles and consider the broader operational flow. Removing barriers to information and idea exchange within an organization is crucial for fostering an environment where innovation thrives and systemic inefficiencies are swiftly addressed.

For an organization to thrive, it's crucial that every team member is aware of the organization's mission and long-term goals. When everyone in the company is aligned with *a clear and consistent purpose*, decision-making becomes more informed, innovation more purposeful, and risks more calculated.

Imagine starting your journey in a company where, from day one, you are immersed in the company's vision and goals. This clarity isn't just a first-day formalism but a daily reinforcement—through meetings, internal communications, and the leadership's actions. This consistent reinforcement helps everyone from the newest recruit to the most seasoned executive to make choices that propel the company forward, ensuring that all efforts are harmoniously aligned with the broader objectives.

Ultimately, the value a business provides is defined by the customer. What customers consider valuable and are willing to pay for dictates the direction and strategies of a business. For a business to sustain itself and grow, it must remain keenly *attuned to the evolving needs and desires of its customers*.

Consider a business that continually engages with its customers, seeking to understand and anticipate their needs. By maintaining this close connection, the business can adapt its offerings to better meet customer expectations, thereby securing its relevance and longevity in the market. It's about more than just responding to needs—it's about anticipating them and innovating in ways that delight and surprise.

These principles form the pillars upon which operational excellence is built, providing a robust framework that guides organizations toward sustainable success.

These cutting-edge principles of Operational Excellence go beyond simple guidelines; they're the backbone of what makes organizations thrive. As you integrate these principles into your strategy, think about customizing each to match your organization's unique ambitions and needs.

Exploring the principles of Operational Excellence has revealed its crucial role for businesses aiming to compete and to stand out in today's rapidly changing market. Before we dive into the strategies that boost operational excellence, let's take a moment to fully grasp and appreciate why mastering this area is vital for any organization.

Operational excellence is a mindset that drives an organization to deliver superior value to its customers. By eliminating waste and inefficiencies, resources are saved and redirected towards enhancing the customer experience. This transformation is about optimizing every operation to enrich value delivery at every customer touchpoint.

Think about the value disciplines model proposed by Treacy and Wiersema, which categorizes market-leading companies according to their dominance in one of three areas: Operational Excellence, Customer Intimacy, or Product Leadership. These companies achieve industry standards in two areas but excel exceptionally in one, thereby setting themselves apart in the marketplace.

Consider Apple, renowned for its product leadership through continuous innovation and high-quality standards. Apple's commitment to exceptional design and user experience places it at the forefront of product innovation. On the other hand, Amazon exemplifies operational excellence by streamlining online shopping to make it as fast, easy, and convenient as possible. This focus enables Amazon to consistently deliver value through efficiency and reliability, securing its market leader status.

Then there's Lowe's, which prioritizes customer intimacy. By deeply engaging with customers to understand and meet their home improvement needs, Lowe's ensures that each customer interaction is both helpful and enriching. This approach boosts customer loyalty and drives sales by providing tailored solutions to customer projects.

Operational excellence stands out as a vital competitive lever. It enables a business to differentiate itself by optimizing its operations to meet both the current and future customer needs effectively. Indeed, operational excellence allows a business to outperform its competitors by being leaner, more efficient, and more responsive to the market dynamics.

This is why operational excellence is a fundamental component of a business's ability to succeed and sustain growth in a competitive landscape.

Structural Changes for The Pursuit of Operational Excellence

Following our exploration of the fundamental importance of operational excellence, it becomes clear that to build a robust foundation for enhanced efficiency and excellence, organizations must sometimes initiate profound structural and technological transformations. This often involves making strategic choices about restructuring teams, centralizing or decentralizing functions, and leveraging advanced technology—each tailored to foster an environment conducive to achieving operational goals.

Initiating a team restructuring is a significant move aimed at aligning your workforce with the strategic objectives of your organization. This step isn't just about changing roles; it's about enhancing how teams function—making them more efficient, effective, and fostering a culture ripe for innovation.

The ultimate goal here is clear: we need our teams' structure and their day-to-day workflows to mesh seamlessly with our long-term ambitions and the everyday demands of our operations. This realignment paves the way for smoother internal communication and simpler, more direct processes. It encourages a spirit of cooperation that breaks down old barriers and ushers in a wave of fresh, innovative thinking. Teams transformed in this way aren't just rearranged—they're reborn, equipped to be more agile and responsive to the ever-evolving landscape of business and market shifts.

The journey begins with a meticulous assessment of the existing team structures. We dive deep to pinpoint where we're falling short or where inefficiencies are holding us back from our true potential. This crucial evaluation lays the groundwork for crafting tailored, innovative team frameworks that are built not only for greater collaboration but also for superior flexibility. These new setups draw from a rich tapestry of diverse skills and viewpoints, significantly enhancing our collective problem-solving capabilities and driving innovation.

But we don't rush these changes across the board. Instead, we opt for a pilot test—a focused trial within a part of the organization that lets us measure the effectiveness of new structures in real-world conditions.

It's a test run that allows for tweaking and fine-tuning based on actual feedback and performance data.

And as we move forward, the transition is supported by *comprehensive training and support systems*. We're committed to fully equipping our team members for their new roles and providing our leaders with the tools they need to successfully guide the dynamics of transformed team

Another critical element in creating a foundation for operational excellence involves the strategic decision to centralize or decentralize organizational functions. This choice is deeply intertwined with an organization's ability to adapt and thrive in various market conditions.

The choice between centralizing and decentralizing various functions within an organization hinges on several factors including the organization's scale, operational complexity, and overarching strategic objectives. Each approach offers distinct advantages and addresses different organizational needs.

Centralization tends to streamline decision-making, standardize processes, and enhance cost efficiencies by consolidating activities and resources in a central hub. This can be particularly effective for functions such as human resources and finance, where uniformity and compliance across the organization are crucial.

Decentralization offers each department or location within a company the ability to make decisions tailored to local conditions and customer needs, fostering a strong sense of autonomy and promoting innovation. Teams that are closer to the action are often more adept at spotting trends and responding swiftly to the changing demands of the market.

When considering the structural approach for an organization—whether to centralize or decentralize—it's crucial to start with a comprehensive evaluation of the organization's needs, both current and anticipated. This assessment should take into account factors like the geographical spread of the company, the complexity of its business processes, and the need for agility in response to market changes.

For many organizations, a hybrid model that incorporates both centralized and decentralized elements proves most effective. This might mean centralizing core functions such as finance and HR to benefit from economies of scale and consistency while allowing branches like sales and customer service to operate independently, thus maximizing responsiveness and closeness to the customer.

Regardless of the chosen structure, the role of technology is indispensable in facilitating robust communication and the seamless flow of information across the company. Implementing advanced technologies, such as enterprise resource planning (ERP) systems and cloud-based platforms, can effectively synchronize centralized planning with decentralized execution, ensuring that the organization remains cohesive yet flexible.

The third critical aspect of creating a formidable foundation for operational excellence is the *integration of advanced technology*. Reflecting on my own journey through various organizational roles, I've witnessed firsthand the transformative impact that technology can have on operational efficiency. It's a pivotal element that can propel an organization forward by automating tasks, enhancing decision-making processes, and encouraging continuous innovation.

The strategic integration of technologies such as Artificial Intelligence (AI), machine learning, and automation tools is about fundamentally enhancing the way your organization operates.

Integrating advanced technologies into an organization transforms how teams work and thrive. By automating both mundane and complex tasks, technology frees up employees to focus on strategic and creative initiatives. This shift boosts productivity and enriches job satisfaction by removing the tedium of repetitive tasks. Moreover, tools like artificial intelligence (AI) and machine learning elevate decision-making to new heights, uncovering insights and patterns that might otherwise go unnoticed.

The journey to technological transformation begins with a thorough mapping of your organization's processes. Identifying which tasks— from data entry to sophisticated analytics—can be automated is the first crucial step. The choice of technology, whether it's AI for enhancing data analysis, IoT devices for real-time monitoring, or blockchain for increased supply chain transparency, should align closely with your operational goals.

Implementing new technologies should start small, with pilot projects. These initial trials allow you to measure the technology's impact in a controlled setting and make necessary adjustments before a full-scale rollout.

However, the introduction of new systems often meets resistance. To navigate this, it's essential to have a solid change management strategy. Comprehensive training programs are crucial to equip your team with the skills needed for these new tools. More than that, involving them in the transition process helps alleviate concerns and fosters an environment receptive to change, ensuring the new technologies are fully integrated and embraced.

By thoughtfully integrating advanced technology into your operations, you can significantly enhance efficiency, reduce costs, and stay competitive in today's fast-paced business environment.

Reflecting on the structural and technological changes we've discussed, it becomes evident that these adjustments are merely the beginning of a continuous journey towards operational excellence. An organization must constantly refine and adjust its operational strategies to remain on the path of excellence, adapting to changing conditions with precision and agility.

Once you have set the foundations with restructuring teams and integrating new technologies, the real work of *ongoing management and improvement* begins. This is where the cycle of monitoring and continuous improvement plays a crucial role in ensuring that these changes yield the desired outcomes and adapt to the evolving business landscape.

To successfully implement new strategies and changes within an organization, it is critical to establish and consistently track performance metrics. These metrics provide tangible benchmarks that not only highlight successes but also pinpoint areas that fall short of expectations.

Alongside these quantitative assessments, establishing robust feedback mechanisms is essential. Gathering insights from employees at all levels offers a valuable perspective on how changes impact the daily workflow and overall morale. This feedback often reveals challenges and issues that might not be immediately apparent through metrics alone.

Moreover, it's important to conduct regular reviews of all recent implementations, from structural adjustments to new technological integrations. These reviews should verify that the changes remain aligned with the organization's strategic objectives and operational demands. Approaching these evaluations with flexibility and a willingness to adapt is crucial. This mindset ensures that your organization remains dynamic and capable of adjusting to evolving internal and external circumstances, thereby maintaining a competitive edge and operational effectiveness.

By embedding these strategies into your operational framework, you ensure that the pursuit of operational excellence is not a one-time project but a perpetual state of evolution. Each step forward is informed by the last, creating a dynamic cycle of improvement that keeps your organization agile and competitive.

The Resilience Integration Framework

As we dive into the architectural shifts necessary for achieving operational excellence, let's introduce a unique framework specifically designed to bolster our resilience in this dynamic business landscape. I've named this framework the Resilience Integration Framework (RIF), which is tailored to enhance our capabilities to withstand disruptions and optimize operations even in the most unforeseen circumstances.

At the heart of RIF is *strategic resource allocation*. This entails fortifying the very core of our operations to ensure continuity and efficiency during unexpected challenges. The process begins with a thorough risk identification and prioritization. We utilize a comprehensive approach to dissect our operational landscape, employing tools like SWOT and PESTLE analyses to map out potential threats meticulously. This detailed examination allows us to not only identify risks but also to understand their origins and potential impacts.

Once risks are identified, we employ a prioritization matrix to categorize them by the severity of their impact and the likelihood of occurrence. This systematic sorting helps direct our resources to the most pressing vulnerabilities, transforming potential weak points into fortified assets. Moreover, by engaging stakeholders from every sector of our organization, we ensure that our strategy benefits from a 360-degree perspective, making our approach as inclusive and robust as possible.

To maintain agility in our operations, we implement flexible resource management strategies that allow us to adapt swiftly to both challenges and opportunities as they arise. We establish a dynamic pool of resources—including both material and human resources—that can be deployed rapidly. Our workforce is trained to pivot seamlessly between roles, enhancing our ability to respond to changing conditions without delay.

Furthermore, we commit to real-time monitoring and adjustment of our resource allocation. This continuous oversight enables us to anticipate and meet needs proactively, ensuring that we are always prepared. Regular scenario planning also plays a critical role. By simulating various crisis situations, we test and refine our readiness, ensuring that our responses to actual events are both swift and effective.

Building a supply chain that is as robust as it is responsive involves crafting a system capable of withstanding global disruptions without faltering. Our objective here is clear: ensure that our supply chain thrives even in the face of unexpected global changes.

We begin by conducting a meticulous assessment and selection of suppliers, prioritizing not only their ability to deliver consistently but also their stability and reliability. By diversifying our supplier base and spreading it across different geographies, we effectively disperse risk and enhance the resilience of our supply chain against localized disruptions. This strategic diversification is critical in creating a supply network that can sustain operations under various scenarios.

Beyond simply acquiring suppliers, we focus on fostering strategic partnerships. These relationships are built on mutual goals and shared commitments to maintain supply continuity, even when unexpected challenges arise. Such partnerships are integral to our strategic approach, ensuring a collaborative effort towards stability and reliability.

To keep our supply chain agile and effective, we engage in continuous monitoring and evaluation. The global supply chain landscape is dynamic, with new risks and opportunities emerging regularly. By maintaining a vigilant watch on both performance and potential risks, we are able to adapt our strategies promptly. This proactive approach allows us to align our operations with emerging trends and insights, ensuring that our supply chain remains both resilient and efficient in tackling the complexities of global trade.

Investment in Robust Process Infrastructure for Operational Excellence

In cultivating a framework for operational excellence, we see that the next crucial aspect of our strategy hinges on robust process infrastructure. This entails equipping our operations to handle unexpected disruptions with agility and steadfastness. Let's explore why robust infrastructure is fundamental to our pursuit of operational excellence and how it can be effectively rolled out to fortify our organization against the ebbs and flows of market dynamics.

A resilient infrastructure enables our organization to swiftly adapt to changes and disruptions. By having systems that can quickly pivot, we minimize downtime and keep our operations running smoothly, which is essential in today's fast-paced market environment.

Investing in streamlined processes and integrating advanced technologies enhances the quality of our output. This improvement in efficiency is crucial for reducing operational overheads and delivering superior quality to our customers, thereby improving our competitive edge.

Strong infrastructure is our frontline defense, safeguarding our core operations against unexpected disruptions and ensuring that we can maintain our commitments without compromise even during unforeseen events.

We strive to elevate our operational capabilities by *integrating cutting-edge technology*, which enhances automation and provides real-time insights essential for efficient and foresighted decision-making. By embedding IoT sensors and employing AI across our operational channels, we are able to monitor and predict potential disruptions. This preemptive approach allows us to address issues before they escalate, maintaining operational continuity. Furthermore, leveraging cloud technology allows us to manage and analyze vast datasets effectively.

This capability is crucial for making informed strategic decisions, optimizing resource allocation, and improving operational agility. Additionally, we develop customized software solutions tailored to meet our unique needs, which enhance functionality and user experience, thereby boosting operational efficiency and adaptability.

In parallel, we focus on *building a fail-safe operational environment* by implementing redundancies and automated systems that ensure continuity. We strategically place redundancies at critical junctures—such as power supply, network connectivity, or data storage—to safeguard against any single points of failure that could disrupt our operations. Our automated failover systems are meticulously designed to transition to backup operations seamlessly, without the need for human intervention, thus ensuring uninterrupted service. Regular testing and diligent maintenance of these systems guarantee that they are always operational, ready to function as expected, and safeguard our operational integrity.

We are committed to *cultivating a culture of continuous improvement* that enhances both process resilience and operational efficiency. By adopting methodologies such as Lean and Six Sigma, we continuously streamline our processes, eliminating waste and reducing variability. This ongoing refinement is crucial in strengthening the overall resilience and efficiency of our operations.

Routine process audits are integral to our strategy, helping us identify inefficiencies and pinpoint areas needing improvement. These audits provide us with a clear roadmap for strategic adjustments and enhancements, ensuring our operations remain aligned with our high standards of efficiency.

Moreover, we place a strong emphasis on employee training and involvement in our continuous improvement programs. By encouraging employees to engage actively, we ensure they are equipped with the necessary skills and feel motivated to contribute to our operational excellence

This proactive approach ensures our operations are protected and are also primed to thrive.

The Role of Leadership in Operational Efficiency

When we discuss the strategic enhancements that drive operational efficiency and excellence, it becomes crucial to consider a defining element of success: leadership. John C. Maxwell eloquently captured the essence of leadership when he stated, "A leader is one who knows the way, goes the way, and shows the way." This reflection on leadership sets the stage for understanding its profound impact on operational efficiency, particularly through the lens of *transformational leadership.*

Transformational leaders stand out for their visionary ability to inspire and chart a path forward. This type of leadership is pivotal for operational excellence, as it involves aligning the organization's strategic goals with innovative practices and processes. By articulating a compelling vision, transformational leaders mobilize the entire organization to transcend personal limits and embrace ambitious goals, thereby driving significant improvements in operational efficiency.

Empowering employees is a core principle of transformational leadership. Leaders who excel in this style create environments where team members feel valued and are encouraged to take initiative. This empowerment leads to increased engagement and ownership, where employees proactively identify inefficiencies, propose solutions, and implement changes that contribute directly to operational excellence. Such an empowered workforce is more agile, responsive, and productive, key traits for maintaining competitive advantage.

Transformational leaders are champions of innovation. They inspire a culture where questioning the status quo is encouraged, and creative thinking is rewarded. This focus on innovation is essential for operational excellence as it propels the development of new processes and solutions that streamline operations and enhance service or product delivery. In environments driven by transformational leadership, employees are inspired to explore innovative ideas that lead to breakthrough performance improvements.

A culture of continuous improvement is the bedrock of operational excellence, and transformational leaders are its architects. They set high standards and motivate their teams to consistently seek ways to exceed these benchmarks. This dynamic approach ensures that the organization continually adapts and evolves, enhancing processes and systems to meet changing market demands and internal growth objectives effectively.

Transformational leadership transforms the very fabric of an organization, making operational excellence a natural outcome of its cultural and strategic endeavors. By inspiring, empowering, and innovating, transformational leaders ensure that their organizations are leaders shaping the future of their industries.

In our exploration of leadership's impact on operational excellence, we've delved into the transformative power of visionary leadership. Now, let's shift our focus to a different but equally critical style—*transactional leadership*. This approach, with its emphasis on clarity and structure, plays a pivotal role in enhancing operational efficiency.

Transactional leadership is marked by its clear delineation of roles, responsibilities, and expectations. This clarity is invaluable in operational settings, as it ensures that every team member knows precisely what is expected of them. By setting explicit goals and performance metrics, transactional leaders create a well-ordered environment where efficiency thrives. Such a framework facilitates a smooth flow of operations and minimizes ambiguities that can lead to inefficiencies.

At the heart of transactional leadership is a straightforward reward and punishment system designed to motivate employees. This approach directly ties performance to tangible rewards or consequences, fostering an environment where high performance is pursued and recognized. Employees are motivated to exceed expectations, knowing that their achievements will be rewarded. Conversely, the potential for disciplinary action for underperformance instills a sense of accountability and deters slack.

Transactional leaders excel in maintaining operational efficiency by focusing on short-term objectives. This concentration on immediate results ensures that daily operations are executed flawlessly, with each task and output optimized for quick wins and immediate benefits. While this may sometimes constrain innovation, it ensures that the organization remains robust and efficient in its current operations, reliably meeting its day-to-day operational goals.

A defining feature of transactional leadership is its emphasis on close supervision and control. Leaders employing this style continuously monitor their teams, ensuring that all activities align with the organization's standards and goals. This vigilant oversight allows for the rapid detection and rectification of any deviation from set procedures, thereby maintaining a high standard of operational efficiency.

While transformational leadership inspires and drives long-term strategic change, transactional leadership is indispensable for its ability to instill order and efficiency in daily operations. The structured environment it fosters is essential for achieving immediate operational goals, ensuring that the organization operates like a well-oiled machine. By integrating the strengths of both transformational and transactional leadership, organizations can achieve a dynamic balance that supports both immediate efficiencies and long-term excellence.

As we tread through the dynamic interplay between leadership styles and their profound impact on achieving operational excellence, we come to the cornerstone of leadership success: strategic decision-making. This aspect isn't just about choosing paths that lead to immediate results; it's about aligning every decision with the ultimate goal of operational excellence. Strategic decisions serve as the guiding stars that ensure every action taken is in harmony with the organization's broader objectives.

The Essence of Strategic Decision-Making in Operational Excellence

Strategic decision-making is pivotal for ensuring that every organizational move aligns seamlessly with its long-term goals. In the realm of operational efficiency, this means making choices that optimize processes, reduce waste, enhance quality, and ultimately, drive the organization towards its envisioned future. Leaders must possess a profound understanding of their organization's mission and strategic objectives, coupled with a keen insight into the operational landscape, to make decisions that prioritize efficiency.

Strategic decisions, particularly the **adoption of Lean management principles**, can dramatically transform operations. Imagine a manufacturing environment where every element of the production line is streamlined to perfection. Techniques like value stream mapping allow organizations to identify and eliminate wasteful practices, enhancing operational flow, reducing costs, and improving output quality. This boosts efficiency amd ensures the organization remains agile and responsive to market demands.

Further, consider the transformative impact of **automation in a service-oriented setting**. Strategic investments in technology, such as deploying chatbots for handling routine customer inquiries, can revolutionize customer service dynamics. This shift allows human agents to focus on more complex, value-added interactions, significantly enhancing service efficiency and customer satisfaction. Additionally, integrating an ERP system can unify disparate business processes, streamline data management, and optimize resource allocation, driving comprehensive operational improvements. Such strategic decisions are pivotal in propelling an organization toward greater operational efficiency.

Efficiency often flourishes in the **fertile ground of collaboration**. A strategic initiative to encourage cross-functional teams to tackle efficiency projects can unearth innovative solutions that a single department might overlook. This streamlines operations across various facets of the organization while nurturing a culture enriched with teamwork and innovation, leading to sustainable operational excellence.

Strategic decisions to integrate customer feedback into operational processes provide invaluable insights that can significantly enhance efficiency. For instance, feedback highlighting prolonged wait times can lead to strategic changes in workforce scheduling or the introduction of self-service options, thus improving both efficiency and customer satisfaction.

One of the most transformative strategies a business can adopt is *Just-In-Time inventory management.* This approach, which aligns perfectly with lean principles, involves receiving goods only as needed in the production process, thereby minimizing the costs tied to excess inventory storage. The strategic implementation of JIT cuts down on unnecessary stock and significantly enhances an organization's agility. By reducing inventory levels, companies can swiftly adapt to changes in customer demand, ensuring that resources are allocated efficiently without compromising the quality of output. This agility becomes a competitive advantage, enabling businesses to respond dynamically to market fluctuations with minimal disruption.

Strategic resource reallocation is another critical decision-making process that significantly enhances operational efficiency. Consider the power of data-driven analysis in uncovering resource imbalances across an organization. For instance, if a company discovers that certain processes are excessively resourced while others are stretched thin, reallocating these resources can harmonize operational flow and eliminate inefficiencies. This might mean diverting funds from traditional, labor-intensive tasks like manual data entry to more strategic initiatives such as customer experience enhancements or digital marketing. By doing so, productivity is optimized and the organization also becomes better positioned to meet its growth objectives effectively.

Scenario planning stands out as a strategic tool that equips leaders to face the future with confidence. This proactive approach involves anticipating possible future events and crafting detailed response strategies. By preparing for various potential outcomes, organizations can shield themselves from future shocks and maintain operational efficiency under different scenarios. This kind of foresight allows companies to stay resilient, ensuring that their operations are efficient today and are robust enough to withstand future challenges. Whether it's an economic downturn, technological disruption, or sudden shifts in consumer behavior, well-prepared organizations can adapt swiftly and maintain continuity in operations.

Strategic decision-making processes stand out as practical and potent tools, propelling businesses towards operational excellence. It's the combination of efficiency, adaptability, and foresight that truly sets the standard for operational excellence in the rapid pace of today's business world.

Developing a Leadership Strategy for Operational Excellence

In our journey toward operational excellence, we find that the essence of leadership involves decision-making and actively shaping an environment that breathes efficiency.Let's explore how leaders can strategically cultivate this environment.

Setting clear efficiency goals acts as a guiding star for organizations, helping them streamline operations, optimize resources, and enhance output quality. These goals serve as benchmarks that encourage teams to reduce waste and improve processes, which are essential for maintaining competitiveness in a dynamic market.

For efficiency goals to be impactful, they must be specific, measurable, achievable, relevant, and time-bound (SMART). This level of clarity ensures that every team member understands exactly what is expected of them and drives their efforts toward achieving these targets. For example, instead of broadly aiming to "reduce waste," a more specific goal would be "to reduce material waste by 15% within the next quarter by implementing recycling protocols and optimizing production layouts."

It is crucial that these efficiency goals align with the organization's overarching strategic objectives. This alignment ensures that every effort to enhance operational efficiency directly contributes to broader business outcomes, such as increasing market share or improving customer satisfaction. This strategic coherence helps in mobilizing all parts of the organization towards a common goal, enhancing overall performance.

To ensure that efficiency goals truly transform operations, leaders must establish mechanisms for continuous monitoring and dynamic adjustment. This involves setting up systems to track progress and integrating feedback loops where employees can report challenges and successes. Such systems allow for real-time tracking and enable leaders to swiftly make adjustments to strategies in response to operational realities. For instance, if a particular efficiency goal is consistently being met ahead of schedule, it might be time to set more ambitious targets, or if a goal is not being met, to investigate the barriers and adapt accordingly.

Building on the foundation of clear efficiency goals, the next critical step for leaders in driving operational excellence is *aligning incentives with these objectives*. This alignment ensures that the motivation of every team member is directly connected to the organization's broader efficiency goals, fostering a culture where everyone's efforts contribute meaningfully to the company's success.

Aligning incentives with efficiency goals boosts morale and enhances productivity by ensuring that employees' personal achievements are recognized and rewarded. This approach encourages a direct connection between individual performance and organizational success, creating a win-win scenario for both employees and the company.

One effective way to align incentives is through performance-based compensation. For instance, implementing bonus schemes that reward employees for meeting or exceeding specific efficiency targets can drive a more focused effort towards achieving these goals. Such financial incentives directly link an individual's contributions to tangible rewards, significantly boosting motivation and productivity. A manufacturing firm, for example, might offer a bonus for reducing machine downtime, directly influencing operational efficiency.

However, it's crucial to recognize that motivation isn't driven by financial rewards alone. Non-financial incentives such as career development opportunities, public recognition, and the creation of a positive and supportive work environment also play a major role in employee engagement. For example, providing employees with opportunities to lead projects or partake in training programs enhances their skills and shows trust and recognition of their potential, further motivating them to excel.

Moreover, the structure of these incentives must be flexible and adaptable, allowing them to evolve in response to changing business needs and goals. This flexibility ensures that the incentive system remains relevant and continues to drive the desired behaviors as the organizational focus shifts over time. It allows leaders to fine-tune incentives to better match the dynamic nature of business operations and market conditions, ensuring that the organization remains agile and responsive.

Discussing the alignment of goals and incentives, we need to reinforce the *cultivation of a robust culture of performance and accountability*. This culture acts as the backbone of operational excellence, ensuring that each member of the organization is aware of their roles and fully engaged in driving success.

A well-established culture of performance and accountability embeds a sense of ownership among employees, encouraging them to take responsibility for their actions and their impact on organizational goals. This culture enhances transparency and propels continuous improvement, essential for maintaining competitive advantage.

The adage "actions speak louder than words" holds especially true in leadership. Leaders must exemplify the performance and accountability they expect to see in their teams. By openly demonstrating these values, leaders set a profound precedent for behavior within the organization. This influence fosters a workplace where accountability is the norm, and striving for excellence is the collective goal.

Clarity is key in promoting a performance-oriented culture. By setting explicit expectations and coupling them with regular, constructive feedback, leaders ensure that every team member understands their role in the broader efficiency goals. Such clarity helps individuals identify areas for improvement and align their efforts more closely with organizational objectives.

Empowering employees goes beyond granting them the autonomy to make decisions—it involves providing the necessary tools, training, and support to excel at their tasks. When employees are trusted to drive change and innovate, they are more likely to engage deeply with their work and push the boundaries of what they can achieve.

Celebrating successes is as important as setting targets. Recognizing and rewarding employees for their contributions to efficiency goals reinforces the importance of these objectives and motivates the team to sustain their high performance. Whether through formal rewards, public acknowledgment, or personal commendations, recognizing employees' efforts bolsters a culture where striving for excellence is valued and pursued.

The synthesis of clear efficiency goals, aligned incentives, and a vibrant culture of performance and accountability is fundamental to any organization's success. Such a strategic framework enhances operational productivity while instilling a pervasive sense of commitment and engagement across all levels of the organization.

Wrapping up our dive into operational excellence, it's key to remember that this isn't the end of the road. The strategies and principles we've talked about are game changers for any organization looking to really nail excellence and keep growing.

Operational excellence is a continuous pursuit that challenges us to adapt, innovate, and lead with intention every day. Whether through the structuring of teams, the strategic allocation of resources, or the empowering leadership styles, each element plays a critical role in crafting a solid operational framework.

As leaders and innovators, the question remains: How will you apply these insights to elevate your operations to new heights? How will you ensure that your pursuit of operational excellence is a permanent fixture of your organizational culture?

Let these questions guide your next steps as you continue to build an environment where efficiency is celebrated, resilience is ingrained, and excellence is the standard.

– 4 –

The Agile Operation

*"Embrace agility to stay ahead, turning challenges
into opportunities for growth."*

In every crisis lies the seed of opportunity—a truth that became strikingly clear during the COVID-19 pandemic. As the world grappled with unprecedented challenges, organizations found themselves thrust into a mode of operation that tested their limits like never before. Leadership faced a barrage of critical decisions, strategies unraveled, and tasks that once seemed essential quickly became obsolete.

In this crucible of uncertainty, a crucial strategy emerged: operational agility. It became evident that companies equipped with agile operations could not just survive but thrive. They were nimble, adjusting their strategies and operations swiftly to continue serving their customers amidst turmoil. Research during and after the pandemic underscored this point: organizations ingrained with agile practices were adapting and excelling, outmaneuvering the chaos to find new paths to success.

We've explored the domain of operational health, efficiency, and excellence. Now, let's dive deeper and explore the essence of operational agility. This is a vital skill for keeping pace in our fast-changing world. We're going to get to the heart of what makes operational agility stand out, why it's so crucial, and how it differs from the broader idea of business agility.

Conceptualizing Operational Agility

Let's start by unpacking the concept of operational agility. Often, when we think about agility in a business context, it's painted with a broad brush—encompassing everything from strategic pivots to cultural shifts. However, operational agility zeroes in on the core functions of a business, sharpening its focus on the ability to adapt and respond effectively at the operational level.

Operational agility represents an organization's capacity to modify its operations swiftly and adeptly in response to changes. This agility is crucial; it's about enhancing how an organization responds to external market forces and internal changes without losing momentum. The goal is clear: maintain high performance and customer satisfaction even as the complexities of the business environment evolve.

Let's break down the key components of operational agility. At its heart, operational agility is about the ability to quickly change operational processes and systems. Whether responding to sudden market changes or internal demands, the agility to pivot is indispensable.

Utilizing cutting-edge technologies and data analytics is no longer optional. These tools are instrumental in enhancing responsiveness and fortifying decision-making capabilities. They transform raw data into insights, guiding the reconfiguration of operations to be more effective.

The dynamic allocation of resources—manpower, materials, or capital—is essential for operational agility. It's about moving resources fluidly and precisely to where they are most impactful, ensuring that the organization can respond to operational demands without delay.

Operational agility is not a set-it-and-forget-it strategy. It involves a constant cycle of evaluating and improving processes. This ongoing refinement is what keeps an organization ahead, ensuring processes are efficient, resilient and responsive to the ever-changing business world

Now that you've grasped the essence of operational agility and its paramount importance, what do you think is the next crucial aspect to focus on? It's general business agility. While both are critical, they shine their spotlight on different layers of an organization's dynamics.

Recognizing this key distinction paves the way for you to harmonize operational tactics with strategic initiatives more effectively.

Operational agility is all about the "how" in the heartbeat of business operations—it's the secret sauce to swiftly and effectively tweaking how things get done. This agility zeros in on making specific processes as efficient and adaptable as possible, often sparked by the urgent needs and quick wins. It's about leveraging technology and fine-tuning processes to make rapid, impactful changes.

On the flip side, think of general business agility as the big-picture game. It's all about the "what" and "why" - figuring out which strategies need a makeover and why it's essential to shake things up to stay in tune with the market's rhythm or to smoothly tread through internal changes. This kind of agility isn't just about quick moves; it's a holistic approach that integrates strategy, operations, and culture, all driven by a vision for staying adaptable not just today, but way into the future. It involves inspiring leaders to make bold decisions, fostering a culture that embraces change, and designing an organization that's flexible enough to bend without breaking.

The components of general business agility include:

Strategic Agility: This is the capacity to quickly and effectively redefine business strategies in response to external market changes. It demands foresight and vision, enabling organizations to seize strategic opportunities promptly.

Organizational Agility: This pertains to how adaptable the organizational structure and culture are. A flexible organization fosters an environment that encourages innovation, collaboration, and proactive responses to change.

Leadership Agility: This involves leaders' ability to anticipate shifts, inspire adaptability among teams, and exemplify navigating through uncertainties. Leaders play a crucial role in steering the organization towards its strategic goals while maintaining operational efficiency.

Let's delve into how these crucial concepts manifest in tangible scenarios. Consider an organization proficient in operational agility—efficient at adjusting production rates, switching between suppliers, or swiftly implementing new technologies. While these are impressive feats, without aligning these operational efficiencies with the strategic goals of the company (a core aspect of general business agility), there might be a risk of resource misallocation or missed strategic opportunities.

On the other hand, a company strong in general business agility might possess visionary leadership and flexible strategies but could falter in translating these into effective operational changes. This discrepancy can lead to inefficiencies at the operational level, hampering the organization's ability to capitalize on strategic initiatives effectively.

By fully grasping and integrating operational and general business agility, organizations can make sure their quick operational changes are both efficient and strategically astute. This positions them to flourish in the fast-evolving market of today. Such integration creates a strong framework where strategic initiatives and operational tactics align, promoting sustained growth and adaptability.

Understanding operational agility in these terms allows us to see it as a distinct, vital element of broader business agility, focusing on the concrete and immediate aspects of an organization's function.

Now that you have a solid understanding of the nuances of operational agility and how it differs from general business agility, let's tackle a question I often encounter: Why is operational agility essential for businesses to remain competitive and responsive in today's fast-evolving market? Let me guide you through this crucial aspect.

Operational agility is paramount in enabling businesses to respond swiftly to sudden market changes. This capability is vital in industries where consumer preferences and technological trends shift frequently. Imagine a scenario where a significant disruption hits your industry. Companies that can adapt quickly are the ones that survive and thrive.

Take the manufacturing sector as an example. Tesla, during the 2020 computer chip shortage, showcased remarkable operational agility. While many competitors faced significant delays due to the scarcity of chips, Tesla redefined its production processes and redesigned its vehicles to use different chips. This quick adaptation allowed them to continue production, keeping pace with market demand and staying ahead of competitors who struggled to adjust.

Moreover, operational agility is crucial for enhancing customer satisfaction. Businesses that can meet customer needs promptly and effectively are the ones that build lasting loyalty. In service-oriented sectors, where customer expectations for speed and quality are particularly high, this agility is a game-changer.

Consider Amazon's operational practices. During peak times like the holiday season, Amazon's ability to rapidly scale operations and logistics is a testament to its agility. By processing and shipping orders quickly, Amazon consistently maintains high levels of customer satisfaction. This capacity to swiftly adapt to fluctuating demand not only meets but often exceeds customer expectations, cementing their loyalty and trust.

Operational agility empowers businesses to stay ahead in a constantly changing environment. It equips them to handle disruptions smoothly, respond to market shifts rapidly, and keep customers delighted. This agility isn't just a competitive advantage; it's a necessity in today's fast-paced business landscape.

As we've seen, the nimbleness afforded by operational agility doesn't just keep businesses competitive—it also significantly enhances their ability to manage risks. In scenarios ranging from economic upheavals to geopolitical tensions or natural disasters, operational agility allows companies to react promptly and effectively mitigate potential disruptions.

A compelling example of this is Pfizer during the COVID-19 pandemic. With a framework of operational agility in place, Pfizer swiftly pivoted its operations towards the development and distribution of a vaccine. By accelerating research, approval, and manufacturing processes, Pfizer played a crucial role in addressing a global health emergency, showcasing how agility can turn responsive action into life-saving impact.

Moreover, operational agility is a powerful driver of innovation. It creates an environment where businesses can quickly test and implement new ideas, essential for maintaining a lead in competitive markets and for exploring new opportunities. Google exemplifies this approach; its operational agility facilitates the rapid development and testing of new products and services. This capability allows Google to regularly introduce innovative solutions to the market, often outpacing competitors and continually redefining technology standards.

Operational agility also brings significant cost efficiency and resource optimization. By enabling businesses to adjust dynamically to changes in supply and demand, it ensures that resources are utilized effectively and waste is minimized. This adaptability is crucial for maintaining cost control and maximizing profitability.

Consider IKEA's approach to inventory management and production processes. IKEA employs advanced forecasting and responsive manufacturing techniques, allowing it to adjust production based on real-time sales data. This agility minimizes overproduction and reduces inventory costs. By producing only what is needed, when it's needed, IKEA saves on storage costs and reduces the risk of excess inventory becoming obsolete.

This resource optimization extends beyond inventory management. Agile operations enable businesses to reallocate resources swiftly to areas where they are most needed, whether it's labor, materials, or technology. This dynamic resource management ensures that every part of the organization is operating at its highest potential, reducing downtime and enhancing overall productivity.

Through these lenses, operational agility transforms from a strategic advantage to an essential pillar of modern business strategy, ensuring organizations are resilient, proactive, and perpetually ahead of the curve.

Characteristics of Agile Operations

Let's take a closer look at the key characteristics of operational agility. This concept is essential for organizations aiming to excel in today's rapidly changing business environment. It includes several core traits—responsiveness, flexibility, and resilience—that allow businesses to adapt quickly and effectively to shifting market conditions, customer needs, and internal challenges.

Responsiveness stands at the heart of operational agility. It's about an organization's ability to react swiftly to customer demands, market changes, or operational disruptions. This trait is crucial for maintaining customer satisfaction and staying ahead of the competition.

One practical way to embody responsiveness is through real-time data utilization. By leveraging real-time data analytics, businesses can monitor trends and performance metrics, making swift, informed decisions. For example, a retail company might use real-time sales data to adjust inventory levels or promotional strategies instantly, ensuring they meet customer demands without delay. This approach keeps shelves stocked with in-demand products and avoids overstocking items that aren't selling.

Establishing customer feedback loops is another critical aspect of responsiveness. Direct channels for customer feedback and integrating this feedback into operations can significantly enhance responsiveness. Using customer relationship management (CRM) systems to track and respond to customer inquiries and complaints promptly ensures that customer needs are met quickly and efficiently. This practice helps businesses adapt their services and products to better align with customer expectations, fostering loyalty and satisfaction.

As Jeff Bezos, the founder of Amazon, once said, "We see our customers as invited guests to a party, and we are the hosts. It's our job every day to make every important aspect of the customer experience a little bit better." This quote highlights the importance of being responsive to customer needs and continuously improving to meet their expectations.

Diving deeper into the heart of operational agility reveals *flexibility* as its bedrock. This capability to morph operations, processes, and strategies effortlessly is vital for flourishing in a fast-evolving business arena. Flexibility empowers organizations to grasp emerging opportunities and deflect risks amidst the tumultuous waves of change.

Consider the approach of modular process design. This strategy reimagines operations as fluid and adaptable, untouched by the constraints of the broader business ecosystem. Picture a manufacturing firm where production lines transform with the ease of a chameleon's color shift, aligning with the ebb and flow of consumer desires. This approach unlocks unparalleled efficiency and empowers companies to adapt to market changes gracefully, eliminating downtime and unnecessary expenses with the finesse of a master tactician.

Adaptive resource allocation stands as the linchpin of operational agility. Imagine the power of dynamically shifting resources—whether human talent, materials, or financial capital—to align with the ever-changing aspects of priorities. Companies achieve operational continuity and seize emerging opportunities with grace. Picture a tech company swiftly gathering project teams to tackle sudden technological breakthroughs or market demands, only to redeploy those resources once the mission is accomplished. This form of agility ensures resources flow to where they spark the most innovation, turbocharging organizational responsiveness and effectiveness.

Embracing these practices, organizations unlock the power of flexibility, a key to swiftly and efficiently treading through the the ever-shifting challenges and opportunities. This dynamic skill set stands as the cornerstone for securing a competitive advantage and propelling towards enduring success.

Now, let's delve into another vital characteristic of operational agility: *resilience.* Resilience is the capacity of an organization to withstand disruptions and recover quickly from setbacks, thereby maintaining continuous operations and safeguarding assets and overall business health.

In day-to-day operations, resilience begins with robust risk management frameworks. Implementing comprehensive risk management strategies that identify potential threats and develop mitigation plans is essential. This involves regular scenario planning and stress testing to prepare for possible disruptions. By anticipating various challenges, organizations can devise proactive measures to mitigate risks before they escalate into significant issues.

For instance, think about how critical it is for a financial services firm to ensure continuous access to customer data. Establishing redundant systems is crucial in this context. By setting up backup data centers, the firm ensures that customer data remains accessible even if one center experiences a failure. This redundancy provides a safety net, allowing the business to continue its operations seamlessly, safeguarding customer trust and business integrity.

Building resilience is all about creating a culture where growth and improvement never stop. It's about looking back at what went wrong and learning from it, ensuring those mistakes don't happen again. Imagine a workplace where everyone is on the lookout for ways to get better, to fix what's weak before it breaks. That's where resilience blooms. It's this relentless pursuit of improvement that makes bouncing back from setbacks faster and paves the way for lasting success.

There is a powerful statement that gets to the heart of what resilience is. Shawn Achor, an inspiring author and speaker once said, "The best leaders are those who reveal their true strength not in the easy times, but in the moments of great challenge." Isn't it what resilience is all about - facing difficulties head-on and coming out stronger on the other side?

When organizations integrate these characteristics of responsiveness, flexibility, and resilience into their everyday hustle, they set themselves up to tackle today's challenges and whatever tomorrow throws their way. These traits allow businesses to quickly pivot to meet market demands, seize fresh opportunities, and bounce back from setbacks—securing their success and sustainability for the long haul.

Agility and Technology

As we delve deeper into the paradigm of operational agility, we must acknowledge that we are living in an AI era, where technological advancements are happening at an unprecedented pace. To truly harness operational agility, businesses need to leverage these advancements effectively.

Cutting-edge technologies such as cloud computing, artificial intelligence (AI), and the Internet of Things (IoT) play central roles in enhancing operational agility by enabling real-time decision-making and adaptability.

Cloud computing is foundational in enhancing operational agility due to its flexibility, scalability, and efficiency. It allows businesses to deploy and scale resources on demand without the upfront costs associated with traditional IT infrastructure.

One of the key advantages of cloud computing is real-time scalability and flexibility. Cloud platforms enable businesses to adjust their resource usage based on real-time demands, ensuring they can handle sudden spikes in data traffic or storage needs without any delay. This capability is crucial for businesses that experience variable workloads, such as e-commerce sites during sales events. By dynamically scaling resources, companies can maintain seamless operations and provide uninterrupted service to their customers.

Enhanced collaboration and mobility are other significant benefits of cloud services. Cloud platforms facilitate seamless collaboration across geographies, allowing teams to access, edit, and share documents anytime, from anywhere. This speeds up project timelines and enhances productivity. In today's globalized business environment, this mobility is particularly beneficial. Teams can work together efficiently, regardless of location, ensuring that projects stay on track and goals are met promptly.

When we discuss the transformative impact of cloud computing on operational agility, we see that it has revolutionized the way businesses operate by offering unprecedented levels of scalability, flexibility, and cost-efficiency. A prime example of this transformation is Netflix.

Netflix, the world's leading streaming entertainment service, has harnessed the power of cloud computing to manage its massive content library and deliver streaming services to millions of users globally. The company transitioned to cloud computing to address the scalability challenges associated with its growing subscriber base and the increasing demand for streaming content.

Netflix utilizes Amazon Web Services (AWS) for its cloud infrastructure, allowing it to dynamically scale its computing resources in real-time. This scalability ensures that Netflix can handle peak traffic loads, such as new season releases of popular shows, without any disruption to service. The flexibility of cloud computing enables Netflix to deploy thousands of servers and petabytes of storage within minutes, meeting the demands of its users across the globe. This real-time scalability and flexibility are critical in maintaining a seamless streaming experience, ensuring that users can enjoy their favorite shows and movies without interruption.

Additionally, the cost efficiency of cloud computing has been a significant advantage for Netflix. The cloud's pay-as-you-go model allows Netflix to optimize its IT spending, converting what would have been a significant capital expenditure into a more manageable operational expense. This cost efficiency has enabled Netflix to invest more in content creation and innovation, further solidifying its market leadership. By reducing the financial burden of maintaining a vast IT infrastructure, Netflix can focus its resources on enhancing its content offerings and improving user experience.

The example of Netflix illustrates how leveraging cloud computing can transform a business, providing the flexibility, scalability, and cost-efficiency needed to thrive in today's digital age.

Let's now delve into another transformative technology: *Artificial Intelligence (AI)*. AI revolutionizes business operations with its ability to automate intricate processes and empower swift, intelligent decision-making. This game-changing technology is transforming inventory management, elevating customer engagements, and streamlining logistics like never before.

In the world of inventory management, the power of AI to sift through mountains of data, spotting trends and forecasting futures, is nothing short of magic. Imagine AI as the ultimate oracle, precisely predicting the ebb and flow of stock levels, and conjuring up replenishment orders with a snap of its digital fingers. This isn't just convenience—it's revolution. Businesses ride the wave of perfect inventory balance, untouched by human hands.

A real-world example of this can be seen with NVIDIA, a leader in AI technology. NVIDIA utilizes AI to manage its inventory more effectively. By implementing AI algorithms, NVIDIA can predict demand for its products with high accuracy, ensuring it meets customer needs without overstocking. This application of AI in inventory management streamlines operations and supports NVIDIA's supply chain resilience, allowing it to respond swiftly to market changes.

Enhancing customer interactions with AI-driven solutions is another area where AI proves invaluable. AI-driven chatbots and virtual assistants revolutionize customer service by handling inquiries and issues in real time. This technology improves customer satisfaction by providing immediate responses and solutions to queries, allowing human customer service agents to focus on more complex and nuanced customer needs, thereby optimizing the allocation of human resources.

A notable example of enhanced customer interactions is Bank of America's virtual assistant, Erica. Erica uses AI to provide personalized banking advice to customers, handling routine transactions and inquiries, which frees up human agents to tackle more complex issues. This enhances customer satisfaction through efficient service and improves the operational agility of the bank by allowing it to allocate resources more effectively.

In logistics and supply chain management, AI enhances operational agility by optimizing shipping routes and delivery methods. This optimization is achieved through predictive analytics, which assesses numerous variables to determine the most efficient routes and schedules.

UPS uses AI to optimize its delivery routes through its ORION (On-Road Integrated Optimization and Navigation) system. ORION analyzes delivery routes in real time, considering factors such as traffic conditions, weather, and the location of packages in the truck. This system helps UPS reduce delivery times and fuel consumption, significantly enhancing its operational agility and environmental sustainability.

Harnessing AI transforms businesses, automating decision-making, revolutionizing operations, and enabling a dynamic response to the ever-evolving challenges and changes.

Following our discussion on AI, let's now explore how the *Internet of Things (IoT)* is transforming business operations. By connecting physical devices across the internet, IoT enables enhanced data collection, analysis, and automated control. This connectivity leads to more responsive and intelligent business operations, significantly boosting operational agility in several key areas.

Real-time monitoring and maintenance are among the most impactful applications of IoT. IoT devices continuously monitor the health of machinery and equipment by collecting data on parameters such as temperature, vibration, and pressure. This predictive maintenance capability is crucial in sectors like manufacturing and logistics, where equipment reliability and uptime are directly tied to operational efficiency and productivity. By predicting potential failures before they occur, IoT allows for timely maintenance, reducing unexpected breakdowns and costly downtime. Moreover, regular monitoring and maintenance based on IoT data can extend the operational life of machinery, leading to significant cost savings on equipment replacement.

Another area where IoT excels is enhancing supply chain visibility. IoT sensors placed on products, pallets, or containers provide real-time data on the location and condition of goods throughout the supply chain. This enhanced visibility is a game-changer for logistics and supply chain management, allowing companies to track assets from production through delivery. Real-time data enables businesses to make immediate adjustments to their logistics strategies, such as rerouting shipments to avoid delays or responding to changes in demand. With better visibility, companies can optimize their supply chain operations to ensure faster and more reliable delivery to customers.

Resource management is another critical area where IoT technology plays a vital role. Sensors can measure consumption rates and identify areas where resources are being wasted, providing data that can be used to optimize usage. Efficient resource management reduces operational costs by minimizing waste and improving overall efficiency. Additionally, by optimizing resource use, IoT supports sustainability initiatives, helping companies reduce their environmental impact.

A real-world example of IoT's impact on operational agility can be seen with Maersk, one of the world's largest shipping companies. Maersk has effectively utilized IoT to enhance its operational agility, particularly in fleet management and route optimization. By equipping its containers with IoT sensors, Maersk gains real-time visibility into the location and condition of its cargo. These sensors track various parameters such as temperature and humidity, ensuring the integrity of sensitive goods during transit. This data allows Maersk to optimize shipping routes by analyzing real-time traffic data, weather conditions, and sea currents, thereby reducing fuel consumption and improving delivery times. Furthermore, the ability to monitor cargo conditions in real time enables Maersk to proactively address any issues that might affect the quality of goods, such as adjusting the container environment or rerouting to faster paths if delays are detected.

Maersk's use of IoT demonstrates how this technology can significantly enhance operational agility by improving supply chain visibility, optimizing resource use, and enabling proactive maintenance and management. As IoT technology continues to evolve, its role in driving operational efficiency and sustainability is expected to grow, offering even more opportunities for businesses to enhance their competitive edge.

Risk Management in an Agile Operation

In the whirlwind of today's business world, where technology leaps and market demands shift with dizzying speed, the mantra of operational agility echoes louder than ever. Enter Agile Operations, or AgileOps—a powerhouse fusion of Agile's swift-footed methodologies and DevOps' seamless techniques. It's a formidable framework that integrates the ethos of continuous improvement deep into the essence of company culture.

AgileOps is particularly adept at embedding risk management into the daily operations and strategic decision-making of an organization. This is vital in today's unpredictable environments where the ability to manage and mitigate risks promptly can dictate a company's success or failure. Agile methodologies, such as Scrum, inherently support risk management through their iterative processes and frequent communications with stakeholders. For example, daily scrums are a feature of the Scrum framework where team members discuss current challenges and obstacles, effectively identifying and strategizing on immediate risk factors every single day.

This methodological framework offers substantial advantages in managing risks:

AgileOps promotes an environment where risks are recognized as they arise and are addressed instantly. This proactive approach to risk management is facilitated by regular sprint reviews and retrospectives, along with the utilization of tools like risk registers and burndown charts. These tools and practices help in tracking risks and assessing their impact continuously, allowing for immediate corrective actions.

Operational agility enables organizations to swiftly adjust their strategies in response to market volatility. This flexibility is crucial for maintaining a competitive edge and fulfilling customer expectations effectively amidst market shifts. The ability to pivot quickly and efficiently reduces exposure to market-related risks and ensures that the organization remains resilient and adaptive.

AgileOps is instrumental in promoting cross-functional collaboration and open communication, which are vital for effective risk management. When teams work together seamlessly, they are better equipped to share insights, identify potential risks early, and develop collective strategies to address them. This proactive collaboration significantly reduces the likelihood of project delays or failures. By breaking down silos and encouraging open dialogue, AgileOps ensures that everyone is aligned and informed, leading to more cohesive and effective risk management.

The iterative nature of AgileOps encourages continuous learning and improvement. Teams are constantly reflecting on their processes and outcomes, learning from past experiences, and adapting to emerging trends. This cycle of continuous improvement refines risk management practices but also enhances the organization's overall risk resilience. By fostering an environment where learning and adaptation are integral,

AgileOps ensures that teams are always evolving, ready to tackle new challenges and mitigate risks more effectively.

Flexibility in resource allocation is another critical advantage of operational agility. AgileOps allows for the dynamic allocation of resources to areas of highest risk or opportunity, ensuring that efforts are concentrated where they can have the most significant impact. This flexibility is crucial in a resource-constrained environment, enabling businesses to adapt swiftly to changing conditions and priorities. By focusing resources on critical areas, organizations can mitigate risks more efficiently and capitalize on opportunities that drive growth and innovation.

Harnessing the power of Agile methodologies and DevOps practices, operational agility transforms an organization's capacity to handle the unpredictable with ease. AgileOps, by integrating risk management into the very essence of daily operations and strategic choices, empowers businesses to not just react, but proactively engage with potential risks. This forward-thinking strategy shields the organization from unforeseen disturbances, boosting its ability to innovate and pivot swiftly in the face of a constantly evolving market.

With our journey through the foundations of operational agility, we've explored the interplay of responsiveness, flexibility, and resilience that characterizes truly agile operations. As we've seen, operational agility is about thriving by continuously adapting and improving.

The insights we've gathered provide a solid groundwork, but as Professor Theodore Levitt wisely pointed out, "Ideas are useless unless used. The proof of their value is in their implementation. Until then, they are in limbo." This statement rings particularly true in the context of operational agility. Knowing what to do is only the beginning; the real challenge—and opportunity—lies in putting these concepts into practice.

As we move forward, we will step out of this conceptual limbo and dive into the practical aspects of implementing operational agility. It's time to move from understanding to action.

– 5 –

Implementing Agile Principles

*"Agile principles transform operations,
making adaptability and innovation part of your core."*

As we find ourslves in the heart of operational agility, let's be mindful of a thought from Anita Roddick: "Speed, agility, and responsiveness are the keys to future success." Now that we understand what agility means at its core, it's time to roll up our sleeves and put these concepts into action.

Agile isn't just for tech anymore. Its principles stretch far beyond software development, reaching into the heart of industries like manufacturing, logistics, and beyond. It's about making every part of your operation quicker, more flexible, and better equipped to respond to rapid change. Let's turn these agile principles from ideas into tools that transform how your operations run, making your workflow truly responsive to market changes.

Agile Methodology Frameworks

Exploring agile methodologies in practice, what better starting point than one of the most popular frameworks? **Scrum.**Scrum has transcended its software development roots to revolutionize how teams tackle complex projects across various industries. Its origin traces back to 1993 when Jeff Sutherland, John Scumniotales, and Jeff McKenna of

Easel Corporation drew inspiration from a Harvard Business Review article by Takeuchi and Nonaka. This article likened innovative product development to rugby, where the game is a series of encounters with the ball, moving back and forth among the team members. They proposed a flexible, holistic product development strategy where a team works as a unit to accomplish a common goal.

At the heart of Scrum's methodology is the concept of iterative development. Unlike traditional project management techniques that aim for a big launch at the end of a lengthy process, Scrum breaks down the project into manageable, bite-sized pieces, each delivering a tangible output. This allows teams to adjust their strategies based on feedback and changing requirements continuously.

Roles within Scrum serve as the backbone of its operational structure. The Product Owner champions the vision of the project, prioritizing tasks based on business value and stakeholder feedback, ensuring the team always focuses on the most impactful tasks. The Scrum Master, more a facilitator than a traditional manager, guides the team through Scrum practices, clears obstacles, and ensures that the team is as productive as possible. The Development Team, typically made up of professionals from various disciplines, collaborates closely to deliver high-quality increments at the end of each Sprint.

The events in Scrum are carefully designed to maximize collaboration and efficiency. Sprint Planning kick-starts the cycle, setting the stage for what will be accomplished. Daily Scrums, quick stand-up meetings, ensure that each day is optimally used and that any issues are quickly communicated and addressed. The Sprint Review and Retrospective foster a reflective approach, allowing the team to look back at their work to celebrate successes and pinpoint areas for improvement, ensuring that each cycle is more effective than the last.

Scrum's artifacts include the Product Backlog, a dynamic list of everything that might be needed in the product, prioritized to guide the team systematically through its workload. The Sprint Backlog narrows this down to the immediate cycle, providing a clear plan for the Sprint ahead. The Increment is the culmination of each Sprint's effort—a complete piece of work adding value to the end product.

This structured yet flexible approach allows Scrum teams not just to react to changes but to anticipate and adapt proactively. It's a way of working that acknowledges the reality of project management: no plan survives contact with reality without the need for adjustments.

Let's delve deeper into how Scrum's methodologies translate into more agile operations that can effectively respond to the unpredictable ebbs and flows of the market.

Firstly, Scrum inspires an environment where collaboration and communication are paramount. Daily Scrums and regular review sessions ensure that every team member is engaged with the project's progress and hurdles. This ongoing dialogue streamlines problem-solving and enhances the cohesion within teams, making it easier to tackle challenges swiftly and effectively.

One of the most significant advantages of Scrum is the agility it instills in teams. By structuring work in short sprints, teams are equipped to adapt quickly to new information or changes in the project's scope. This adaptability is crucial in today's fast-paced business environments, where being able to pivot quickly can be a key differentiator.

Continuous improvement is another cornerstone of Scrum. Through Sprint Retrospectives, teams are encouraged to reflect on their workflow, successes, and areas where they can improve. This cycle of reflection and adaptation gradually enhances the overall process.

Scrum also accelerates the time to market. By delivering work in increments, products or enhancements can be released progressively, ensuring that the market receives new offerings faster. This method streamlines feedback loops and allows businesses to be more responsive to consumer needs, staying ahead of the competition.

Transparency and visibility in Scrum come from its structured roles, artifacts, and ceremonies. Everyone from team members to stakeholders has a clear insight into the project's progress and potential bottlenecks. This visibility supports better decision-making and ensures that all parties are aligned on the project's objectives and outcomes.

Focusing on the customer, Scrum prioritizes development efforts according to the backlog items that hold the most value to the customer.

This customer-centric approach ensures that the team works on features that offer the most return while increasing customer satisfaction and loyalty by consistently addressing their most pressing needs.

Consider the impact of Scrum on companies like John Deere and Bosch. At John Deere, Scrum has shortened development cycles, improved cross-functional collaboration, and raised the bar on product quality. These enhancements mean quicker responses to market demands and superior product offerings. Similarly, Bosch's adoption of Scrum has revolutionized their project management by allowing for more experimental approaches in their hardware development, driving innovation and efficiency.

Through these examples and the principles of Scrum, it's clear that operational agility is truly about smart, strategic adaptations that keep businesses competitive and aligned with their markets.

After exploring Scrum's dynamic influence on operational agility, it's compelling to pivot to another agile methodology that has significantly shaped how industries manage workflow and efficiency—**Kanban.** Originating in the factories of Toyota in the late 1940s, Kanban was created by Taiichi Ohno as a lean method to enhance manufacturing processes. It introduced a just-in-time production system that revolutionized inventory management and set the stage for a broader application across various sectors.

Kanban has evolved from its automotive roots to a staple in the world of software development and beyond, thanks to David J. Anderson's adaptation in the early 2000s. The beauty of Kanban lies in its simplicity and visual nature. At its heart is the Kanban board, a tool that captures the essence of workflow visualization. This board is typically divided into columns such as 'To Do,' 'In Progress,' and 'Done,' each populated with cards that represent work items. As these cards transition from one column to the next, they mirror the journey of tasks from initiation to completion. This visual method provides teams with immediate insights into work status, progress, and bottlenecks, facilitating quick decision-making and adjustments.

Kanban's emphasis on transparency transforms operations by ensuring that every team member has a clear understanding of workflow and task status. This visibility is crucial for enhancing communication and collaboration, which are foundational to operational agility. Moreover, Kanban introduces the concept of limiting work in progress (WIP). By capping the number of active tasks, Kanban helps teams focus on completing current assignments before taking on new ones, which significantly cuts down multitasking and operational overload.

Flow management is another cornerstone of Kanban. Teams are encouraged to monitor their work's progression continuously, making it easier to spot delays and holdups. This ongoing scrutiny allows for quicker optimizations and smoother workflow, ensuring that projects start strongly and finish successfully.

Kanban also demands clarity in process policies. Teams need to establish explicit rules for task advancement and completion, which standardizes procedures and reduces ambiguity. This clarity is complemented by regular feedback loops—such as daily stand-ups and periodic retrospectives—which foster a culture of continual improvement. Each session provides an opportunity to refine strategies, tweak processes, and ensure that the team's approach remains aligned with evolving project demands and market conditions.

The evolutionary nature of Kanban encourages teams to implement changes incrementally, based on real performance data, which mitigates risk and promotes gradual adaptation rather than disruptive overhauls. This methodical approach to innovation has proven effective across various fields, from technology firms optimizing software releases to manufacturing units refining production lines.

Incorporating Kanban into operational processes is about building a responsive, adaptable, and continuously improving workflow. Whether it's a tech startup or a manufacturing giant, the principles of Kanban offer a pathway to enhanced agility and sustained competitiveness in a constantly evolving business environment.

While exploring the nuances of Kanban, it becomes increasingly clear how this methodology significantly boosts an organization's operational agility.

At Toyota, Kanban was a paradigm shift. The company faced significant challenges in managing inventory levels and ensuring timely production to meet fluctuating market demands. By adopting Kanban, Toyota introduced a visual management system that used physical cards—kanban cards—to signal the need for new supplies, aligning inventory with real-time demand. This just-in-time production minimized waste and optimized resource utilization, allowing for a streamlined process that could adapt quickly to changes.

The continuous improvement culture, or Kaizen, that Toyota embraced under Kanban, played a critital role. It wasn't just about keeping the production line moving; it was about constantly seeking ways to make it move better, faster, and more efficiently. This iterative process of feedback and adaptation led to dramatic enhancements in production efficiency, significantly reducing lead times and improving cycle times.

The real-world implications of Toyota's Kanban application are profound. The methodology's effectiveness in boosting operational agility is evident through:

Increased Efficiency: The meticulous application of Kanban led to sharper production processes, reducing delays and enhancing the overall output rate.

Reduced Waste: Aligning production with actual demand meant that Toyota could cut down on excess inventory, minimizing waste substantially.

Enhanced Flexibility: The agility to adapt to market conditions and consumer demand kept Toyota competitive, enabling them to respond swiftly and effectively to any external pressures.

This transformation at Toyota stands as a strong proof to Kanban's potential beyond its original domain. It highlights the methodology's universal applicability and effectiveness across various sectors, whether in manufacturing, software development, or any area that demands a flexible and responsive operational strategy. Kanban enables organizations to visualize their workflow, manage work-in-progress effectively, and boost collaboration—qualities that are crucial in the modern fast-paced markets.

The Agile Team Composition Framework

Having explored the agile frameworks, we now approach a critical element in adopting these methodologies and ensuring operational agility within an organization: the formation of agile teams. At the heart of agile teams lies the principle of cross-functionality, which is crucial for fostering a dynamic and responsive environment. To guide us through this process, I'll introduce the Agile Team Composition Framework, which serves as a blueprint for constructing teams that are empowered to handle the fast-paced demands of today's business.

This framework is designed around several core principles that emphasize the synergy between diverse skills and the unified focus towards common goals. The essence of agility in teams begins with cross-functional collaboration. Agile teams bring together individuals from various functional areas such as development, design, testing, business analysis, and operations. This diversity inspires a holistic approach to project development and problem-solving, ensuring that all necessary perspectives are considered and that solutions are comprehensive and robust.

Autonomy and self-organization are also fundamental. Agile teams thrive in environments where they are given the freedom to manage their workflows and make decisions independently. This autonomy is supported by a flat organizational structure that encourages quick decision-making and reduces bottlenecks typically associated with hierarchical systems. It also instills a sense of ownership and accountability among team members, driving them to achieve excellence.

Customer-centricity stands at the forefront of the agile mindset. Teams are continuously aligned with the needs and expectations of the customer, ensuring that every iteration of the product or service exceeds customer expectations. This focus helps in maintaining a clear direction and purpose, driving teams to deliver value efficiently.

In this environment, each role is tailored to facilitate project success:

Product Owner

The Product Owner is the crucial link between the team and stakeholders, ensuring that all efforts align with customer needs and business goals. In non-software companies, this role can be adapted to manage any project or product development. For example, in a manufacturing firm, the Product Owner could oversee the creation of a new product line, ensuring it meets market demands and company objectives. They prioritize tasks in the product backlog, determining which ones will have the most significant impact, ensuring efficient and effective project progression.

Scrum Master or Agile Coach

The Scrum Master or Agile Coach plays a vital role beyond simple facilitation. They empower the team, coaching them to optimize their processes for the best outcomes. In non-software companies, this role is equally essential. For instance, in a retail business, the Scrum Master could help teams streamline their inventory management processes or improve customer service workflows. They navigate through challenges, ensuring agile practices are followed effectively, leading to improved efficiency and productivity.

Development Team

The Development Team is composed of experts from various fields who work collaboratively to deliver high-quality results every cycle. In non-software environments, such as a construction company, the development team might include architects, engineers, and project managers working together to complete a building project. Their diverse skills cover everything from initial planning to final inspections, ensuring that the project runs smoothly and meets all standards.

Subject Matter Experts (SMEs) and Specialists

Certain projects require specialized knowledge, which is where Subject Matter Experts (SMEs) and specialists come into play. In non-software settings, such as a healthcare organization, SMEs might include medical professionals who provide critical insights into developing a new patient care protocol. These experts bring in-depth knowledge and specific skills that enhance the team's overall capabilities, ensuring that every aspect of the project is handled with precision and expertise.

This structure and the roles within it are not just placeholders but pivotal in steering the team towards agile success. However, it is essential to remember that the team's structure and dynamics are equally crucial in this framework.

Agile teams thrive when they are kept relatively small, typically ranging from 5 to 9 members. This size ensures effective communication and collaboration while allowing for flexibility and quick decision-making. When dealing with larger projects, it's practical to divide the workforce into multiple sub-teams or squads. Each sub-team should focus on a specific area or component of the product, but they must maintain cross-functional collaboration and alignment through coordination mechanisms such as Scrum of Scrums or shared backlogs. This approach ensures that even as the team scales, the agile principles of collaboration and efficiency are preserved.

Stability within teams is paramount. Avoiding frequent changes in team composition is crucial because it takes time for team members to develop trust, establish effective communication patterns, and reach high-performance levels. Stable, long-lived teams foster a sense of ownership, shared understanding, and continuous improvement. This stability allows teams to delve deeper into problem-solving and innovation, leveraging their collective experience and knowledge without the disruption of constant reorganization.

Collaboration and communication are the lifeblood of agile teams. Implementing agile practices and ceremonies, such as daily stand-ups, sprint planning, and retrospectives, is vital for fostering collaboration, transparency, and continuous feedback loops. These practices ensure that everyone is on the same page, obstacles are swiftly addressed, and the team continuously learns and improves. Utilizing agile tools and techniques like user stories, story mapping, and kanban boards can significantly enhance the visualization and management of the team's work, promoting a shared understanding of tasks and priorities.

Promoting psychological safety within the team is another critical element. It's essential to create an environment where team members feel comfortable taking risks, expressing opinions, and admitting mistakes without fear of negative consequences. This safety net encourages innovation, as team members are more likely to propose bold ideas and solutions when they know their contributions are valued and respected.

Aligning the team's goals and priorities with the overall organizational objectives and strategic direction is crucial for maintaining coherence and purpose. Facilitating effective communication and collaboration between the team and stakeholders ensures that everyone is working towards a common vision. Regular reviews and adjustments of the team's priorities based on changing organizational needs or market conditions help in staying relevant and responsive.

Following this comprehensive framework enables organizations to build agile teams that are cross-functional, collaborative, and focused on the customer. These teams can quickly deliver value, while promoting a culture of continuous improvement and adaptability.

Leadership at the Helm of Agility

While discussing the nuances of agile frameworks, it becomes evident that the linchpin for successfully embedding agility within an organization is its culture. And at the core of fostering a culture that genuinely embraces agility is transformative leadership. So, let's explore how different leadership styles uniquely support agile principles, integrating them intyo daily operations and strategic decision-making.

In an agile environment, **catalyst leadership** shines by focusing on empowerment. Catalyst leaders provide their teams with the necessary resources and information, allowing them the freedom to make decisions. This approach builds trust and value among team members, sparking innovation and agility. These leaders clearly articulate a vision and align team efforts with organizational goals, helping individuals understand the importance of their roles within larger objectives. Additionally, catalyst leaders are adept at facilitating rather than directing, empowering teams to self-organize and collaborate effectively. This is crucial for removing obstacles and streamlining processes.

Parallel to this, **servant leadership** enhances the agile framework by prioritizing the development and well-being of team members. This approach fosters a nurturing environment where individuals feel supported and valued, encouraging them to experiment and innovate. Servant leaders build strong, empathetic relationships that promote a safe space for risk-taking and open communication. They also emphasize community and teamwork, which are critical for sustaining collaboration and mutual support across agile teams.

Lastly, **adaptive leadership** is crucial in navigating the uncertain waters of modern business. Adaptive leaders encourage flexibility and responsiveness, preparing their teams to shift gears quickly in response to new challenges and opportunities. They promote a culture of continuous learning, where ongoing education and adaptation are the norms. By endorsing experimentation and viewing failures as learning opportunities, they cultivate an environment where innovation is both encouraged and celebrated.

These leadership styles, though varied, all share a common goal: to create a dynamic, responsive, and innovative culture that embodies the principles of agility. They make sure agile practices are more than just implemented—they're a way of life for the organization. This nurtures a resilient and adaptive business that's ready to thrive amidst competition and change. Through these leadership approaches, organizations can unlock their teams' full potential, leveraging their collective skills and insights to handle complexities with agility and confidence.

Fostering a Culture of Innovation

True to what we have seen, leadership is instrumental in cultivating a culture of agility. However, equally vital is fostering an innovative mindset throughout the organization. This approach supports and amplifies the impact of agile methodologies, transforming the very essence of how a company operates.

Innovation thrives in environments where experimentation is encouraged and learning from outcomes—both good and bad—is a fundamental process. By empowering teams to undertake small, safe-to-fail experiments, organizations can diminish the stigma associated with failure. This mindset encourages a proactive approach to innovation, where every setback is viewed as a stepping stone towards greater achievements. It is crucial for organizations to adopt a perspective where mistakes are dissected not for assigning blame, but for extracting valuable lessons that pave the way for future improvements.

The implementation of continuous feedback loops is another cornerstone in this architecture of innovation. Regular retrospectives and inclusive stakeholder feedback sessions become invaluable. These gatherings are not mere formalities but are vital tools for ongoing adaptation, ensuring that every team member is heard and that every insight is leveraged to refine processes and outputs.

At the heart of a truly agile organization lies the growth mindset—a belief in continuous development and a curiosity that drives exploration beyond current boundaries. Encouraging this mindset involves not only recognizing and fostering curiosity but also investing in the professional growth of each team member. When staff are provided with opportunities to expand their knowledge and skills, the whole organization advances.

Aligning these innovative endeavors with the strategic goals of the organization ensures that all efforts are coherent and synergistic. By setting clear, attainable goals that resonate with the organization's broader vision, leaders can channel the creative energies of their teams towards outcomes that foster growth and ensure relevance.

A tangible example of these principles in action can be seen in Spotify's agile transformation. By adopting the Squad model, Spotify created a framework that supported autonomous, cross-functional teams dedicated to specific aspects of the service. This model was complemented by a structure of Tribes, Chapters, and Guilds, which facilitated alignment and knowledge sharing across the company. Continuous feedback mechanisms and the agile iteration of features allowed Spotify to refine its service continually, enhancing user satisfaction and maintaining its competitive edge in the dynamic music streaming industry.

Organizations can achieve sustained growth and success in an unpredictable world by embedding these principles into their DNA.

Defining KPIs and Metrics to Measure Operational Agility

Having explored the importance of instilling a culture of agility through leadership and innovation, it's now essential to understand how to measure this agility effectively.

As we have seen, operational agility enables an organization to swiftly adapt its processes, technology, and procedures in response to changing market demands and expectations. However, the ability to adapt must be measurable to ensure that the changes are effective and aligned with the organization's goals. This is where Key Performance Indicators (KPIs) and metrics come into play. These metrics provide actionable insights into the organization's performance and help leaders make informed decisions.

The first core principle for defining KPIs and metrics is **alignment with strategic goals.** It's crucial that the KPIs reflect the organization's broader objectives. For example, if a company's strategic goal is to enhance customer satisfaction, then a relevant KPI might be the average resolution time for customer complaints. This alignment ensures that the efforts to enhance operational agility are directly contributing to the company's overarching mission.

Relevance and specificity are also vital. KPIs should address the specific operational challenges and processes unique to the organization. For instance, in a manufacturing company, KPIs might include production cycle time or defect rates. These specific indicators provide clear, actionable insights that can drive meaningful improvements.

Furthermore, KPIs must be **quantifiable and measurable**. This means using numerical values, percentages, ratios, and other measurable units. Quantifiable KPIs allow for objective assessment and comparison over time. For example, tracking the percentage decrease in time taken to bring a product to market over successive quarters can provide a clear measure of improved operational agility.

A balanced approach to KPIs is essential to ensure a comprehensive view of operational performance. This involves considering various aspects such as efficiency, quality, customer satisfaction, and innovation. For example, while tracking production efficiency is important, it's equally crucial to measure customer satisfaction to ensure that the efficiency improvements are not compromising product quality or customer experience.

Continuous monitoring and adaptation of KPIs are necessary to keep them relevant and effective. As business conditions, market demands, and organizational priorities evolve, so too should the KPIs. Regular reviews and adjustments ensure that the metrics remain aligned with the current strategic goals and provide ongoing value in guiding decision-making processes.

Having explored the foundational principles of these metrics, we see that their real value lies in strategic implementation and use across the organization. This involves a series of thoughtful steps to ensure these tools effectively drive the agility and responsiveness that modern businesses require.

Defining Clear and Measurable Goals is the cornerstone of effective KPI implementation. Each key performance indicator should be tied to specific, measurable targets that reflect the organization's strategic aims and operational needs. This clarity doesn't just simplify performance measurement; it ensures that every part of the organization is aligned towards common objectives, facilitating a unified approach to agility.

Utilizing Agile Tools and Technologies effectively transforms raw data into actionable insights. Modern project management tools like Jira, Trello, and Wrike offer robust capabilities for tracking and visualizing KPIs, making it easier for teams to keep a pulse on performance and progress. These tools also support real-time dashboards and comprehensive reports that help demystify complex data for all stakeholders, ensuring that insights are accessible and actionable.

Regularly Reviewing and Updating Metrics ensures that the organization remains responsive to both internal performance and external market dynamics. Agile ceremonies such as sprint reviews and retrospectives provide ideal opportunities for this evaluation, allowing teams to discuss KPIs in the context of current performance and evolving objectives. This adaptability is crucial for staying relevant in a rapidly changing business environment.

Communicating Metrics Effectively is key to ensuring that everyone in the organization understands what the KPIs are saying and why they matter. Effective communication involves clear, concise presentations of data, often visualized through graphs, charts, and dashboards that simplify complex information. This clarity supports better decision-making and helps align team efforts with strategic goals.

Encouraging Collaboration and Accountability involves making KPI tracking and analysis a team-oriented process. By involving everyone in the KPI discussions, organizations can foster a sense of shared responsibility for the outcomes. This collaborative approach enhances engagement and ensures that team members feel part of the successes and challenges, driving them to actively participate in problem-solving and innovation

Now that we've examined the methods for creating effective KPIs to gauge operational agility, it's time to dive into specific indicators that truly encapsulate an agile operation. These KPIs are essential for monitoring performance and driving meaningful improvements across various organizational processes.

Cycle Time is one of the most direct measures of operational efficiency. It tracks the duration from the start to the completion of a process, providing insights into the speed and efficiency of operations. For instance, in product development or order fulfillment processes, a shorter cycle time often signifies a quicker response capability to market changes, directly enhancing competitive edge and customer satisfaction.

Lead Time takes a broader view, encompassing the total time from when a process is initiated until it is completed. This metric includes all aspects of the process, including both active work and periods of inactivity. By reducing lead time, companies can significantly enhance their responsiveness to customer demands and market changes, which is a direct reflection of operational agility.

Throughput measures the rate at which a company can produce output over a given period and is particularly relevant in manufacturing and service delivery contexts. An increase in throughput usually indicates a rise in productivity and operational efficiency, reflecting well on the agility of the process management.

Work in Progress (WIP) limits are crucial for managing and maintaining the flow of operations. By limiting the amount of unfinished work, organizations can prevent process bottlenecks and overloading, ensuring a smoother workflow and quicker turnaround times.

First-Pass Yield (FPY), an essential quality metric, indicates the effectiveness of the process design and execution by measuring the percentage of products or services that meet quality standards on the first attempt without needing rework. High FPY rates reduce waste while increasing the overall speed and efficiency of production.

Defect Rate measures the frequency of errors or defects in the output and serves as a critical quality control metric. Lower defect rates are indicative of more refined processes and higher product quality, which in turn boosts customer satisfaction and loyalty.

Customer Satisfaction (CSAT) scores provide direct feedback from end-users about their satisfaction with products and services. High CSAT scores are often a clear indicator of an organization's ability to meet or exceed customer expectations, a direct outcome of operational agility.

Employee Engagement is an often overlooked but critical aspect of operational agility. Engaged employees are more likely to be proactive, solve problems innovatively, and adapt to changes swiftly, all of which are essential traits for maintaining agility.

Innovation Rate reflects the organization's capacity to implement new ideas and improvements. High rates of innovation demonstrate a proactive stance towards market demands and challenges, underpinning a culture of continuous improvement.

Time to Market measures the speed with which new products can move from conception to market, a vital metric in today's fast-paced business environments. A shorter time to market typically signals a company's agility in responding to new opportunities or threats.

Operational Cost Efficiency looks at how well resources are being utilized in relation to the output produced. Enhanced cost efficiency signifies that the organization is not only agile but also effective in managing its resources to produce maximum output.

Resource Utilization rates help organizations understand how effectively they are using their assets. Optimizing resource utilization is a critical aspect of maintaining operational efficiency and agility, ensuring that all available resources contribute to productive outcomes.

Together, these KPIs form a solid framework for measuring and enhancing operational agility. They allow leaders to monitor, assess, and adapt their strategies continuously, ensuring that the organization remains agile, efficient, and aligned with market dynamics and customer needs.

Wrapping up our dive into agile principles and how to put them into play, it's pretty evident that being agile is a transformative force. It completely flips the script on how companies operate, especially in a world that never stands still. When organizations get cozy with agile methods, like Scrum and Kanban, and nurture leadership and cultures that really get agility, they're laying down the groundwork for success that sticks around.

Yet, understanding these frameworks and strategies is only the beginning. The true test of operational agility lies in its execution and the tangible outcomes it delivers. What does this look like in practice? How do companies across different industries apply these principles to gain a competitive edge and drive innovation? As we move forward, we will explore the answers to these questions.

– 6 –

Transforming Operations Through Agility

"Agility in operations drives transformation,
unlocking potential and enhancing performance."

As we peel back the layers of operational agility, I'm reminded of Malcolm Gladwell's insightful observation: "Practice isn't the thing you do once you're good. It's the thing you do that makes you good." This idea propels us into the real-world applications of operational agility, where theory meets practice, and strategies are tested against the rigors of daily challenges.

One compelling narrative that epitomizes this journey is the transformation of **Haier,** a global giant in consumer electronics and home appliances. Let's start with their story. Based in China, Haier has redefined the integration of information technology within its operations to stay ahead in a fiercely competitive market. By developing a robust IT infrastructure, Haier has not just upgraded its technological capabilities but has also fostered a culture of rapid responsiveness.

This strategic overhaul enabled real-time data collection and analysis, which in turn, empowered Haier to make swift decisions that align closely with evolving market demands and customer expectations. Such agility is not merely about speed but about precision and adaptability—qualities that Haier has harnessed to enhance its operational efficiency and secure a competitive edge.

The seamless integration of IT across various departments has streamlined internal communications and also strengthened collaboration. This interconnectedness is vital for sustaining agility as it ensures that every segment of the company is aligned and can react cohesively to external pressures.

Now that we have an overview of Haier's journey of operational agility, let's zoom in on its path. Before Haier embraced agile operations, the company grappled with a traditional hierarchical structure that impeded swift decision-making and stifled innovation. Encumbered by layers of management, the organization struggled with inefficiencies and a sluggish response to market dynamics. This rigid, bureaucratic setup hindered internal workflows and the company's ability to connect meaningfully with customers, leaving valuable feedback and insights untapped.

Moreover, Haier's operations were marked by a distinct lack of cohesion, with departments functioning in isolation. This siloed approach to business operations curtailed effective communication and collaboration, essential components for a responsive and adaptable enterprise. Additionally, the company's processes were inflexible, presenting significant challenges in adapting to the fast-paced changes of the global market and evolving consumer preferences.

Transitioning to agile operations, Haier initiated a profound transformation, central to which was the implementation of a robust IT infrastructure. This strategic move facilitated real-time data collection and analysis across various functions, dramatically enhancing decision-making and enabling rapid adjustments to processes based on actionable insights.

Perhaps the most revolutionary change was the adoption of the RenDanHeYi model. This approach decentralized the organization into over 4,000 self-managed micro-enterprises, each functioning as an autonomous unit with its own decision-making authority and profit accountability. This radical restructuring unleashed entrepreneurial spirit and innovation while closely aligning operational activities with customer needs.

Emphasizing a customer-centric approach, Haier leveraged its powerful internet platforms to foster collaboration with a wide array of stakeholders including suppliers, customers, and even competitors. This open, collaborative approach proved instrumental in integrating customer feedback directly into product development and operational refinement.

Additionally, the integration of IT systems across departments eliminated previous silos, enhancing communication and collaboration throughout the company. This interconnectedness enabled Haier to respond more cohesively to market changes, driving efficiency and adaptability.

As we delve deeper into Haier's transformative journey towards operational agility, it's important to spotlight both the tangible benefits reaped and the challenges diligently tackled along the way.

Haier's shift to agile operations markedly enhanced its responsiveness to market fluctuations and customer needs, significantly boosting its competitive edge and customer satisfaction. This newfound agility enabled Haier to adapt swiftly to changing market demands, ensuring they remained at the forefront of industry innovation.

Innovation flourished under the decentralized, self-managed structure, where a customer-centric approach was not just encouraged but ingrained. This environment nurtured the development of innovative products specifically tailored to meet evolving customer preferences, thereby enriching the customer experience and expanding market reach.

Operational efficiency saw remarkable improvements as well. The integration of sophisticated IT systems streamlined processes across the board, minimizing waste and maximizing resource utilization. This operational refinement not only enhanced productivity but also contributed to sustainability by reducing excess.

Moreover, the implementation of the Rendanheyi model revolutionized employee engagement. By empowering employees to take ownership of their work and operate with a high degree of autonomy, Haier cultivated a robust entrepreneurial spirit within its workforce.

This empowerment translated into higher motivation levels, increased job satisfaction, and improved productivity across the organization.

However, the path to this agile transformation was not without its hurdles. Cultural resistance presented a significant challenge. The shift from a rigid, hierarchical structure to a fluid, decentralized model was met with skepticism and resistance from segments of the workforce. Overcoming this inertia required tactful management and a clear communication of the benefits that these changes would bring.

Effective change management was crucial. Haier had to develop and implement strategies that not only facilitated this drastic organizational change but also minimized disruption to ongoing operations. This involved extensive training programs, workshops, and continuous communication to ensure all employees were on board and aligned with the new agile philosophy.

Furthermore, as Haier ventured into this new territory, the need for talent acquisition and development became apparent. Building a workforce that could thrive in an agile environment meant investing in new talents and significantly enhancing the skills of existing employees. This talent transformation was essential to sustain the innovative and agile culture Haier aspired to cultivate.

Through this in-depth analysis, it's clear that while the journey towards operational agility was challenging, the enduring benefits—enhanced responsiveness, innovation, operational efficiency, and employee empowerment—have decisively transformed Haier into a more agile, competitive, and forward-thinking enterprise.

As we shift our focus to another intriguing tale of transformation, let's delve into the story of **Thales**, a global powerhouse in aerospace, defense, and security. Thales's journey from traditional methods to operational agility underscores the critical importance of adaptability in today's complex and rapidly evolving markets.

Before Thales embraced agile methodologies, the company was firmly rooted in the traditional waterfall approach to project management. This rigid, sequential development process often resulted in prolonged cycle times and delayed feedback, constraining Thales's ability to respond swiftly to technological shifts or changing market demands. With each phase of a project dependent on the completion of its predecessor, any delays were compounded, pushing project timelines further.

Compounding this challenge was the structure of Thales's teams and processes. Departments operated in isolation, leading to fragmented efforts that compromised efficiency and effectiveness. This lack of integration not only slowed down the development process but also impacted the overall quality and innovation of solutions provided to customers.

Moreover, adhering to stringent regulations, Thales grappled with high operational costs and recurring quality issues. Discrepancies often surfaced late in the development cycle, necessitating extensive and costly rework. This not only strained resources but also delayed product releases, putting Thales at a competitive disadvantage.

The regulatory space added another layer of complexity. Ensuring compliance with a myriad of international standards and regulations across different markets often slowed down processes and added bureaucratic overhead. Recognizing these challenges, Thales committed to a radical transformation towards agility.

Thales began its agile transformation by implementing the Scaled Agile Framework (SAFe), which brought agility across the enterprise. This structured approach to Lean-Agile practices enabled the company to improve quality and speed of delivery. To ensure a smooth transition, Thales invested significantly in training and change management, training over 800 employees and engaging change agents to guide the organization through this shift.

The company also implemented several Agile Release Trains (ARTs) and one value stream, which facilitated continuous delivery and integration of solutions. This approach allowed for more frequent and reliable releases, enhancing the company's ability to respond to market changes swiftly. Additionally, Thales integrated DevOps practices to align development and production environments, crucial for simulating in-flight systems and ensuring successful deliveries without actual flight testing.

In the Surface Radar TU Processing department, Thales adopted Large Scale Scrum (LeSS) to transform into an agile organization. This involved creating multidisciplinary teams that worked on various specialized subdomains, improving collaboration and reducing defects. The combination of these agile methodologies created a robust framework that significantly enhanced Thales's operational agility.

Adopting agile operations brought numerous tangible benefits to Thales. One of the most significant was the reduction in software release cycle time by more than 30%, enabling the company to introduce new releases twice as fast as before. This acceleration was complemented by improved quality, as the ability to spot bugs sooner and implement continuous integration practices led to a 20% reduction in solution rework.

Cost efficiency also saw a notable improvement. The cost per size point was lowered by 25%, demonstrating significant savings through more efficient processes and reduced rework. Agile practices improved collaboration and transparency across teams, leading to better alignment and more cohesive project execution. This enhanced collaboration, in turn, fostered higher employee engagement and satisfaction, as the agile approach encouraged a sense of ownership and continuous improvement.

However, the transformation was not without its challenges. Transitioning from a traditional waterfall approach to Agile required overcoming cultural resistance. Thales addressed this by investing in comprehensive training and engaging change agents to facilitate the transition. Coordination across specialized teams, particularly in the Surface Radar TU Processing department, posed another challenge. Managing dependencies and improving cross-component knowledge helped Thales overcome this hurdle.

Ensuring regulatory compliance while adopting agile practices was a significant challenge due to the diverse regulations Thales had to adhere to. The company managed this by focusing on fixed solution intent for regulatory requirements and addressing variable factors later, ensuring that they maintained compliance without compromising agility.

Thales's journey towards operational agility highlights the significant benefits and challenges of adopting agile methodologies in a complex, highly regulated environment.

Now, let's shift our focus from the skies to the storefronts, diving into **Zara**'s revolutionary story. Here's a brand that's become a byword for fast fashion and lightning-fast responses, showing us all how operational agility can truly transform the game.

Initially, Zara grappled with the conventional woes of the fashion industry. Operating under traditional fashion cycles with seasonal collections, the company was ensnared by long lead times and sluggish responses to rapidly changing fashion trends. This traditional approach often left Zara trailing behind the swiftly evolving preferences of its customer base.

Compounding these challenges were siloed operations. Design, production, and distribution divisions functioned independently, creating bottlenecks that stifled Zara's ability to act swiftly on market shifts. This disjointed operation structure led to pronounced inefficiencies and delayed the brand's response times significantly.

Moreover, Zara's capacity to gather and incorporate customer feedback directly into its design and production processes was considerably restrained. This limitation was a significant hurdle in an industry where success heavily relies on quickly capturing and responding to consumer trends.

Inventory management was another critical challenge. Zara faced frequent overproduction or stockouts due to outdated demand forecasting methods and elongated production cycles, leading to either surplus inventory or missed sales opportunities.

Zara's adoption of agile operations marked a significant turning point. Embracing vertical integration, the company took control of every facet of its supply chain from design to distribution. This shift enabled better coordination across various departments and slashed lead times and enhanced the brand's flexibility to adapt to market demands swiftly.

At the heart of Zara's transformation was a staunch commitment to a customer-centric approach. Store managers and sales associates became the brand's eyes and ears, gathering nuanced data on customer behaviors and preferences directly from the shop floor. This valuable information was rapidly relayed back to the design and production teams, ensuring that customer insights were quickly translated into actionable strategies.

Investment in smart factory initiatives brought a new level of sophistication to Zara's operations. Automation and real-time data systems were deployed across manufacturing units to provide complete visibility into the production process. This technology enabled Zara to quickly identify production bottlenecks and accelerate the manufacturing of trending items.

Moreover, Zara revolutionized its supply chain to be distinctly agile, characterized by smaller production runs and frequent stock updates based on real-time sales data. This strategy significantly minimized the risks associated with overproduction and stockouts.

The use of cutting-edge technologies such as artificial intelligence (AI) and data analytics transformed decision-making at Zara. AI algorithms anticipated fashion trends and optimized inventory levels, while analytics informed product placements and pricing strategies, markedly enhancing customer satisfaction.

Now, let's delve into the tangible benefits and challenges Zara encountered and overcame on its journey toward operational agility. Zara's shift to operational agility brought numerous advantages. One of the most significant benefits was the drastic reduction in lead times. The company mastered the ability to design, produce, and deliver new garments to stores within just 15 days. This remarkable turnaround time allowed Zara to stay at the forefront of fashion trends, meeting customer demands almost instantaneously.

Improved inventory management was another notable benefit. With an agile supply chain and real-time data systems, Zara could manage its inventory with greater precision. This improvement meant reducing excess stock and minimizing stockouts, which not only led to substantial cost savings but also significantly boosted operational efficiency.

Customer satisfaction soared as Zara closely monitored customer feedback and preferences. By aligning its products more closely with customer needs, Zara fostered higher levels of customer satisfaction and loyalty. This customer-centric approach ensured that the products on offer were exactly what customers desired, enhancing their shopping experience.

Furthermore, Zara's ability to swiftly respond to fashion trends and offer exclusive, limited-quantity products created a sense of urgency among shoppers. This strategy drove higher sales and profitability. Additionally, Zara's minimal reliance on traditional advertising, instead leveraging word-of-mouth marketing, contributed to cost savings and increased profit margins.

The transition to an agile operational model wasn't without its hurdles. One of the primary challenges Zara faced was cultural resistance within the organization. Shifting from a traditional approach to a more agile, responsive model required a significant change in mindset. Zara addressed this challenge by investing heavily in training programs and fostering a culture of continuous improvement and innovation. This investment helped ease the transition and build acceptance of the new agile practices.

Another challenge was the need for enhanced coordination across various departments, such as design, production, and distribution. Initially, these departments operated in silos, which hindered effective collaboration and communication. To overcome this, Zara implemented interconnected systems and promoted a collaborative culture among teams, ensuring that all departments worked seamlessly together towards common goals.

Balancing speed and quality was a persistent challenge. Rapid production cycles can sometimes compromise product quality, but Zara managed to address this by implementing rigorous quality control measures. By leveraging advanced technology to streamline production processes, Zara was able to maintain high standards of quality while still achieving rapid turnaround times.

The challenges they faced and overcame underscore the importance of cultural alignment, effective coordination, and maintaining quality standards in an agile transformation.

Lessons Learned in Applying Operational Agility

These three stories of operational agility serve as powerful lessons on how to integrate agility into the very essence of operations, shedding light on crucial strategies for businesses eager to boost their adaptability. Diving into these stories helps companies spot tactics and practices to make their operations more flexible and responsive to change, paving the way for enhanced efficiency and a stronger competitive edge. Let's understand the implications from this deep dive for other businesses looking to become more agile.

The journey towards operational agility requires a comprehensive approach, starting with a robust investment in IT systems. This foundational step, as demonstrated by Haier, equips businesses with the real-time data analysis and decision-making capabilities essential for swift and informed responses to dynamic market conditions.

Transitioning from traditional hierarchical structures to a more decentralized operational model is another critical strategy. This shift, exemplified by Haier's adoption of the RenDanHeYi model, fosters a culture of entrepreneurship and innovation within smaller, autonomous teams. It's about empowering these teams to make decisions and respond quickly, which significantly enhances overall responsiveness and efficiency.

A customer-centric approach is equally vital. Zara's strategy of integrating real-time customer feedback into every stage of product development and operations ensures that businesses remain closely aligned with market demands and consumer preferences. This ongoing engagement with customer insights facilitates rapid adaptation and fosters greater customer satisfaction and loyalty.

Effective change management is crucial in tackling the transition to agile operations. Thales' comprehensive training and the engagement of change agents illustrate the importance of preparing and supporting employees through this transformation. Ensuring that everyone in the organization understands and embraces agile practices is essential for overcoming resistance and achieving a seamless integration of new methodologies.

Moreover, the implementation of scaled agile frameworks, like SAFe, provides a structured path for adopting Lean-Agile practices across an enterprise, streamlining the process and aligning various elements of the business towards common objectives. The introduction of practices such as Agile Release Trains and DevOps in companies like Thales highlights the benefits of continuous delivery and integration, which are pivotal in reducing cycle times and enhancing the quality of outputs.

However, adopting agile operations is not without its challenges. Companies often face cultural resistance and must manage the delicate balance of innovating quickly while maintaining high quality and meeting regulatory compliance. The experiences of Thales and Zara show that addressing these challenges involves investing in the right technologies and processes while creating a culture of continuous improvement and learning. This culture encourages experimentation, embraces failures as learning opportunities, and continuously refines and optimizes processes.

How Can Businesses Sustain Operational Agility in the Long Run?

Diving into the stories of Haier, Thales, and Zara, we discover something incredible: the transformative impact of operational agility and, even more crucially, the need to keep it thriving. This brings us to the concept of sustainable agility. For organizations eager to integrate operational agility into their very essence, the goal goes beyond simply reaching agility. It's about keeping that agility alive, kicking, and evolving over the long term.

To sustain operational agility, organizations must inspire a culture of continuous learning and adaptation. This involves encouraging a mindset geared towards embracing change and driving innovation. Cultivating such a culture means promoting an environment where questioning the status quo is welcomed and where employees are motivated to take calculated risks. This could involve setting up dedicated innovation labs or teams, which act as incubators for new ideas and facilitate rapid experimentation and prototyping.

Moreover, providing ample resources and tools that enable employees to innovate is crucial. This could range from access to cutting-edge technology to partnerships with academic institutions or startups that bring fresh perspectives and expertise. By investing in these resources, organizations not only fuel creativity but also demonstrate their commitment to innovation as a core business strategy.

Incorporating agile methodologies is another cornerstone of maintaining long-term agility. By adopting frameworks such as Scrum, Kanban, or SAFe, organizations can enhance their team's collaboration and flexibility. These methodologies advocate for iterative development and emphasize the value of customer feedback, which together foster a responsive and adaptive operational environment. Breaking projects into shorter sprints allows teams to remain agile, adapting quickly to new information and changing market demands without being bogged down by traditional long-term planning cycles.

Building upon the foundational strategies for sustainable operational agility, it is crucial to highlight the transformative role of technology and data analytics. In today's digital era, leveraging advanced technologies is a necessity for maintaining long-term agility.

Integrating automation and artificial intelligence (AI) into operations revolutionizes how businesses function. Automation streamlines tedious, repetitive tasks, freeing up human resources for more complex problem-solving activities, while AI brings sophisticated data analysis capabilities that can predict market trends, optimize inventory levels, and even personalize customer interactions. Such technologies enhance decision-making and boost operational efficiency significantly.

The implementation of real-time data systems stands out as a game-changer. By collecting and analyzing data as events occur, organizations can gain instant insights into their operations, identify potential bottlenecks, and adapt processes dynamically. This real-time responsiveness is key to staying agile in a fluctuating business environment, allowing companies to swiftly tackle challenges and seize opportunities as they arise.

Moreover, technology enhances collaboration across organizational silos. Utilizing modern collaborative tools and platforms facilitates seamless communication and knowledge sharing among teams, regardless of their physical locations. This interconnectedness is vital for inspiring a unified approach to innovation and problem-solving, ensuring that all parts of the organization are aligned and moving towards common goals.

Embracing a comprehensive digital transformation is also critical. This doesn't merely involve upgrading old systems but rethinking and integrating various business processes to create a fully connected and transparent operational landscape. Such an integrated approach provides a holistic view of operations and enables organizations to make swift adjustments based on comprehensive, real-time data.

Maintaining long-term operational agility also demands a flexible and adaptive organizational structure. Promoting cross-functional teams is a crucial first step. By enabling collaboration across various departments, companies can enhance communication, reduce bottlenecks, and create a culture of shared responsibility. These teams, composed of diverse skill sets, work together towards common goals, ensuring that different perspectives are considered in decision-making processes.

Empowering self-managing teams takes this concept further. By granting these teams the autonomy to make decisions and adapt processes as needed, organizations can foster a sense of ownership and accountability among employees. Self-managing teams are more agile and responsive, able to pivot quickly in response to changing circumstances without waiting for top-down directives. This empowerment not only boosts morale but also leads to more innovative and efficient problem-solving.

Aligning strategy with agility is another vital component. Agile strategic planning involves regularly revisiting and adapting strategic plans based on current market conditions and internal feedback. This continuous reassessment ensures that the organization remains aligned with its long-term goals while maintaining the flexibility to pivot when necessary. It's about harmonizing the need for a clear, long-term vision with the ability to take immediate, agile actions. Balancing long-term strategy with short-term agility is equally critical. Organizations must set clear, long-term objectives that guide their overall direction while allowing for flexibility in tactical execution.

This balance ensures that while the organization remains focused on its broader mission, it can also respond effectively to immediate challenges and opportunities. It requires a mindset that values both stability and adaptability, recognizing that the ability to pivot quickly is as important as having a steadfast direction.

As we continue exploring the pillars of sustainable operational agility, it's crucial to recognize the importance of investing in employee development and engagement. To maintain agility, organizations must equip their teams with the necessary skills and create an environment where innovation thrives. Continuous learning and upskilling are vital components of this strategy. Organizations should provide ongoing training to equip employees with the latest skills and knowledge. This can include cross-functional training, mentorship programs, and access to external courses and certifications. Encouraging knowledge sharing within the organization is equally important. Regular workshops, seminars, and collaborative platforms can facilitate the exchange of insights, best practices, and lessons learned among employees.

Creating a supportive environment is essential for enhancing employee engagement. Recognizing and rewarding innovation, offering opportunities for career growth, and ensuring a healthy work-life balance can significantly improve employee satisfaction and motivation. Engaging employees in decision-making processes, especially regarding changes in processes or the adoption of new technologies, helps gain their buy-in and reduces resistance to change. When employees feel their opinions and contributions are valued, they are more likely to embrace new initiatives and work collaboratively towards common goals.

Implementing robust performance metrics and feedback loops is another critical aspect of maintaining operational agility. Establishing clear Key Performance Indicators (KPIs) allows organizations to measure the success of their agility initiatives. Regular monitoring of these metrics helps track progress and identify areas for improvement. Using data-driven decision-making ensures that strategic decisions and operational improvements are guided by accurate and relevant information. Collecting and analyzing data on various aspects of operations enables organizations to make informed decisions and optimize their processes.

Adopting a continuous improvement approach is essential for maintaining operational excellence and agility. Regularly reviewing and refining processes based on feedback and performance data helps organizations stay responsive to changes and challenges. Creating channels for open feedback from employees, customers, and other stakeholders is crucial for this continuous improvement cycle. Using this feedback to make necessary adjustments and improvements to processes and strategies ensures that the organization remains agile and capable of adapting to evolving market conditions.

Integrating these strategies helps organizations boost their operational agility and keep it up over the long haul. This way, teams are ready for the challenges right in front of them and for whatever the future throws their way. It's all about staying one step ahead in the fast-changing world of business and keeping that competitive edge sharp.

After discussing the importance of maintaining operational agility over the long term, I'd like to delve deeper and provide some insights into the emerging trends poised to significantly impact operational agility in businesses.

AI and ML are revolutionizing the way businesses operate, offering tools for predictive analytics that can forecast market trends, customer behavior, and operational bottlenecks. For instance, AI-driven predictive maintenance can anticipate equipment failures, thereby reducing downtime and maintenance costs. This level of foresight allows organizations to plan proactively rather than reactively, ensuring smoother operations and better resource management.

Moreover, Intelligent Automation (IA), which combines Robotic Process Automation (RPA) with AI, is set to handle increasingly complex tasks, making data-driven decisions and continuously improving operational efficiency. This integration is expected to streamline workflows, minimize human error, and enhance decision-making processes, ultimately boosting operational agility. Businesses that harness these technologies can expect to see significant improvements in efficiency, accuracy, and speed.

Agile business models are becoming essential for organizations striving to remain competitive and responsive. One such model is the Platform Operating Model (POM), which decentralizes operations and enhances scalability. POMs bring together funding, people, and assets to create platforms that deliver shared products and services across the enterprise. This model eliminates duplication, supports rapid scalability, and enhances customer value delivery.

For example, a bank implemented a POM with agile cross-functional teams, resulting in a 40% reduction in delivery times and a 10-15% reduction in running costs. This demonstrates how POMs can streamline operations and drive significant efficiency gains.

Another emerging trend is Everything as a Service (XaaS), which provides on-demand access to software, infrastructure, and platforms. This model reduces upfront costs and allows businesses to scale resources as needed, enhancing operational agility and efficiency. By adopting XaaS, companies can quickly adapt to changing market demands without the burden of large capital investments.

Having talked about operational agility in the long term, I would also like to add a little primer on the emerging trends that can significantly influence operational agility in the balance.

AI and ML are revolutionizing the way businesses operate, offering tools for predictive analytics that can forecast market trends, customer behavior, and operational bottlenecks. For instance, AI-driven predictive maintenance can anticipate equipment failures, thereby reducing downtime and maintenance costs. This level of foresight allows organizations to plan proactively rather than reactively, ensuring smoother operations and better resource management.

Moreover, Intelligent Automation (IA), which combines Robotic Process Automation (RPA) with AI, is set to handle increasingly complex tasks, making data-driven decisions and continuously improving operational efficiency. This integration is expected to streamline workflows, minimize human error, and enhance decision-making processes, ultimately boosting operational agility. Businesses that harness these technologies can expect to see significant improvements in efficiency, accuracy, and speed.

Building on the innovative potential unleashed by artificial intelligence and cloud computing, agile methodologies such as Scrum and Kanban continue to redefine operational agility. These methodologies support iterative development, promoting an environment where collaboration thrives and adaptability becomes a daily reality. This iterative approach does not just enhance productivity; it significantly shortens the time required to deliver substantial value to customers, aligning perfectly with the rapid pace of market changes today.

Simultaneously, the agility offered by cloud computing is transforming the operational capacities of organizations. Cloud technology provides unparalleled scalability and flexibility, allowing teams to adjust their resources swiftly as project demands fluctuate. This adaptability is crucial in maintaining pace with business and technological shifts without the delays traditionally associated with infrastructure expansion or overhaul.

Moreover, the emergence of serverless computing has revolutionized development processes by removing the need to manage servers, thereby enabling teams to concentrate more on creating value through core business functionalities. This shift not only speeds up development cycles but also enhances operational efficiency by focusing talent on innovation rather than maintenance.

Industry-specific Cloud Platforms (ICPs) represent another stride towards refining operational agility. These platforms deliver tailored cloud solutions that address unique industry challenges, combining multi-cloud services with robust data management and cutting-edge technologies. ICPs not only streamline operations but also offer cost efficiencies and bolster data security, providing a competitive edge in a crowded marketplace.

Organizations that embrace these changes and invest in creating a culture that prioritizes agility and innovation are best positioned for success in an ever-evolving business environment.

As we wrap up the exploration on our journey through operational agility, we've peeled back the layers to reveal the strategies, technologies, and game-changing insights that form the backbone of agile businesses. We've journeyed through stories of innovation, resilience, and an unwavering commitment to adaptability, witnessing firsthand how agility redefines the very culture of organizations.But now, let's dive into the next big thing this book is all about: efficiency.Harvey Mackay once wisely said, "Don't equate activity with efficiency." This prompts us to ponder: what really makes for operational efficiency?

In the upcoming chapters, we delve into the essence of efficiency. We'll explore proven strategies and insights that enhance operational efficiency. Get ready to understand the foundational aspects of operational efficiency and discover practical, actionable hacks that'll totally change how you see and boost your operational efficiency.

CHAPTER

– 7 –

Cultivating Efficiency: Mindset, Culture, and People

*"Efficiency thrives in a culture of continuous improvement
and a forward-thinking mindset."*

We've learned a lot on this journey, and now, as we reach the final stretch, we're perfectly placed to dive into the details of efficiency. Clarence W Barron, the famous Financial Editor and Publisher, once said, *"Everything can be improved."* This idea is at the heart of our discussion now as we zoom in on operational efficiency and the ways it can get better.

At the heart of this exploration are three fundamental pillars: mindset, culture, and people—each interconnected to form the backbone of operational efficiency. Let's delve into how these pillars support and enhance organizational processes.

The Three Pillars of Operational Efficiency

The **mindset** within an organization sets the stage for its approach to efficiency. It is the mental wiring that encourages employees at all levels to look critically at their workflows, identify inefficiencies, and propose enhancements. This efficiency mindset is about nurturing an environment where experimentation and innovation thrive. It empowers employees to develop new solutions that significantly enhance productivity and adaptability—key traits in today's ever-evolving business world.

At the **cultural** core of efficient operations lies the Lean philosophy. Lean isn't just a set of tools; it's a culture that permeates every layer of an organization. It's about relentless waste elimination—identifying redundancies and inefficiencies and systematically removing them. But more than that, Lean culture is about engaging everyone in the journey toward continuous improvement. It's about standardizing processes to ensure consistency while retaining the flexibility to adapt swiftly to new challenges and opportunities. This dual focus helps solidify the foundation upon which operational efficiency is built.

Efficiency is ultimately delivered by **people**. Leaders play a crucial role by providing vision and direction, modeling the commitment to continuous improvement. They are the architects of a supportive environment where resources and tools are readily available to foster innovation and streamline operations. Beyond leadership, the engagement of every employee is vital. When employees are motivated, involved in decision-making, and given opportunities to grow their skills through targeted training and mentorship, they become the engine driving efficiency. Their daily actions and decisions weave the fabric of an organization's operational success.

This triadic relationship between mindset, culture, and people creates a synergistic effect that propels operational efficiency to new heights. As we move forward, we will explore each of these pillars in greater depth, uncovering the strategies that lead to efficiency and the challenges that must be tackled along the way.

The Efficiency Mindset

As we've laid the groundwork for understanding the primary role of mindset in operational efficiency, let's delve deeper into what I refer to as the "efficiency mindset." This mindset isn't just a preference for order over chaos; it's a comprehensive philosophy that pervades every level of an organization, shaping decisions and guiding actions towards maximizing efficiency and value.

Central to an efficiency mindset is an unwavering commitment to continuous improvement. This involves a constant, relentless pursuit to refine and enhance every process. In this environment, the status quo is always under scrutiny, and the pursuit of improvement is perpetual, driving the organization to adapt, innovate, and excel continuously.

Efficiency requires looking beyond the boundaries of individual roles or departments. It demands a holistic perspective that considers the entire operational ecosystem. With an efficiency mindset, individuals and teams are encouraged to transcend their silos and collaborate extensively. This broader view helps unearth inefficiencies hidden in the interconnections of processes, ensuring that improvements are impactful across the entire value chain.

In the context of operational efficiency, intuition takes a backseat to data. An efficiency mindset leans heavily on concrete, empirical evidence to drive decisions. This involves systematically collecting and analyzing relevant metrics to understand cycle times, resource utilization, and process performance. Decisions based on data are more likely to lead to effective solutions, as they address real, quantifiable issues rather than assumed problems.

Lean principles, which emphasize eliminating waste and creating customer value, are deeply ingrained in an efficiency mindset. This involves identifying and removing non-value-adding activities, streamlining processes, and optimizing resource allocation to deliver products or services with minimal waste. It's about maximizing value creation while minimizing unnecessary expenditures.

Recognizing that change is a constant, an efficiency mindset encourages adaptability and agility. Organizations must remain agile to stay competitive, and this mindset fosters the adoption of flexible processes and systems that can quickly respond to market shifts, customer demands, or technological advancements. This ensures that efficiency is maintained even in dynamic and rapidly changing environments.

The importance of an efficiency mindset for operational efficiency cannot be overstated. By eliminating waste and optimizing resources, organizations can significantly reduce costs, leading to improved profitability and competitiveness. Streamlined processes enhance productivity, allowing employees to focus on value-creating tasks and increasing overall output. Efficient operations often lead to improved quality, as standardization, clear communication, and effective control mechanisms reduce errors and defects. In today's competitive business world, operational efficiency can be a significant differentiator, enabling organizations to respond quickly to market changes, offer competitive pricing, and deliver superior value to customers.

Moreover, an efficiency mindset inspires a culture of continuous improvement and empowerment. When employees are encouraged to identify and address inefficiencies, they feel valued and engaged, leading to increased job satisfaction and a more motivated workforce. By optimizing resource utilization and minimizing waste, an efficiency mindset also contributes to environmental sustainability and organizational resilience, reducing the environmental impact of business activities and enhancing the ability to withstand economic or market disruptions.

With a clear understanding of the foundation and significance of the efficiency mindset, let's explore strategies for leaders to model and cascade this mindset throughout the organization. Effective communication, leadership behaviors, and policy adjustments are essential components in this endeavor.

The journey to cultivating an efficiency mindset within an organization starts at the top. To start, *communication* is the cornerstone of embedding an efficiency mindset. Leaders need to articulate what efficiency means for the organization and how it aligns with overall goals. It's about more than just cost reduction or speeding up processes; it's about enhancing productivity and ensuring customer satisfaction at every touchpoint. This vision must be communicated consistently and clearly through various channels—emails, intranet posts, video messages, and in-person meetings—to reach every corner of the organization. Engaging in two-way communication is crucial. Creating opportunities for dialogue through town hall meetings, Q&A sessions, and regular team meetings ensures that employees can ask questions, provide feedback, and share their ideas on improving efficiency. This fosters a sense of ownership and collective responsibility toward achieving efficiency goals.

Leading by example is another powerful strategy. Leaders must embody the efficiency they wish to see in their teams. This means being punctual, prepared, and focused during meetings, making data-driven decisions, and continuously seeking ways to improve their efficiency. Demonstrating these behaviors sets a tangible standard for everyone to follow. Moreover, active listening is a critical component. By understanding the challenges employees face and gathering insights on potential improvements, leaders build trust and show that they value their employees' input.

Adopting a coaching mindset is also essential. Leaders should focus on developing their team's skills and improving performance by providing regular feedback, setting clear development goals, and offering support and resources for continuous learning. Encouraging accountability by setting clear expectations and recognizing those who contribute to efficiency improvements is key. This approach fosters a culture where employees feel empowered and motivated to enhance their performance.

Self-awareness and adaptability are equally important. Leaders must be aware of their strengths and weaknesses and understand how their actions influence the culture and mindset of their employees. Being adaptable and open to change, leaders can adjust strategies based on feedback and evolving circumstances, ensuring that the efficiency mindset remains relevant and effective.

Building on our exploration of how leaders can model and promote an efficiency mindset through communication and behavior, it's equally important to consider the structural underpinnings that sustain these efforts: policy adjustments. These adjustments are critical in anchoring the efficiency mindset into every corner of an organization, ensuring that it translates into actionable and sustained practice.

One effective strategy is the *implementation of balanced scorecards*. These tools help maintain a holistic approach to operational efficiency by measuring not just cost-related metrics but also factors affecting customer satisfaction and employee engagement. By integrating such diverse metrics, organizations ensure that efforts to improve efficiency don't undermine other crucial business aspects.

Additionally, **crafting incentive programs that reward efficiency** can profoundly motivate employees. When people see tangible benefits—be it through bonuses, public recognition, or professional growth opportunities—for their contributions to efficiency, it drives a deeper commitment to the organization's goals.

Training and development also play a key role. Continuous educational programs that focus on skills like lean management, process optimization, and data analytics empower employees to identify inefficiencies and suggest practical improvements. Moreover, mentorship programs can cultivate a supportive environment where experienced staff guide newcomers and less experienced colleagues through the nuances of efficient operations.

On the procedural front, **creating standardized processes** ensures consistency and quality across operations, setting a baseline from which improvements can be measured and scaled. However, it's vital to balance these standardized procedures with the flexibility to adapt to new information or shifting market demands, thus maintaining agility within the framework of standardization.

The cultural aspect of an organization is also a powerful lever for sustaining efficiency. By embedding **efficiency as a core value within the company's broader mission** and daily practices, it becomes a living, breathing part of organizational life. Encouraging a culture that not only values efficiency but also innovation and smart risk-taking can lead to groundbreaking improvements and durability in competitive markets.

Lastly, **establishing robust feedback mechanisms** ensures that the drive for efficiency is continually aligned with the realities of the work environment. Regular feedback loops, from surveys to informal check-ins, allow for the real-time calibration of strategies and processes. This feedback, when coupled with a system that values contributions from all levels of the organization, reinforces a dynamic and responsive approach to operational efficiency.

By putting these policy changes into play, organizations can create an environment where thinking efficiently becomes second nature in daily activities. This holistic strategy makes sure that being efficient is a dynamic habit that evolves and expands along with the organization.

Cultivating a Lean Culture

Now, we are at the second pillar of operational efficiency - culture. Specifically, we are talking about cultivating a Lean culture. To truly understand and implement a Lean culture within an organization, it's essential to grasp the core principles of Lean, including Kaizen (continuous improvement). These principles work together to foster an environment of continuous improvement, waste elimination, and enhanced operational efficiency.

At its heart, Lean culture is all about maximizing value while minimizing waste. *Lean principles*, defined by James P. Womack and Daniel T. Jones, are designed to streamline processes, improve efficiency, and deliver more value to customers. The fundamental principles of Lean include defining value from the customer's perspective, mapping the value stream to identify and eliminate waste, creating flow to ensure smooth processes without interruptions, establishing pull to produce only what is needed when it is needed, and pursuing perfection through continuous improvement.

Kaizen, a cornerstone of Lean, emphasizes continuous improvement through small, incremental changes rather than large, radical transformations. The term "Kaizen" means "good change" or "improvement" in Japanese, reflecting its focus on proactive problem-solving and constant enhancement. In a Lean culture, Kaizen involves all employees in the improvement process, creating a sense of ownership and accountability. By empowering everyone to contribute, Kaizen fosters higher engagement and motivation, driving a culture where identifying and solving problems is part of the daily routine. This approach ensures that improvements are sustainable and less disruptive, leading to steady progress over time.

Exploring Lean culture further, let's focus on two key principles that boost operational efficiency: Just-in-Time (JIT) and Jidoka. Both are crucial for creating a workspace that maximizes value and cuts down waste.

Just-in-Time (JIT) is a management philosophy that profoundly impacts production systems by ensuring products are manufactured and delivered precisely when needed, in the exact quantities required, without excess. This approach not only eliminates the need for large inventories but also aligns production schedules directly with customer demand, ensuring a rapid response to market needs without overproduction. The essence of JIT lies in its core principles which span across total quality management, efficient production, and strategic inventory control, promoting an operational ethos where every element of the production process is synchronized for peak efficiency. This synchronization dramatically reduces waste and costs, while increasing the organization's agility and responsiveness to changes in customer demand.

Jidoka, or "automation with a human touch," is another cornerstone of Lean that integrates quality into every step of the production process. This principle empowers machines and operators to detect anomalies early and intervene immediately, halting production if necessary. The dual focus of Jidoka is not just on identifying defects but on empowering employees to take corrective action swiftly, ensuring that problems are addressed at their root. This empowerment enhances responsibility among workers, turning each employee into a quality inspector and inspiring a profound sense of ownership over their work. The implementation of Jidoka in a manufacturing setting means that quality checks are no longer relegated to final inspections but are an integral part of the daily operations, significantly enhancing product quality and reducing the cost and time associated with reworks.

Both JIT and Jidoka are instrumental in promoting a Lean culture that prioritizes efficiency, quality, and continuous improvement. They encourage organizations to be more adaptive, responsive, and customer-focused, fundamentally shifting how value is perceived and delivered. When you integrate these principles into the very essence of your organization, you'll see better operational efficiency, happier employees and more loyal customers.

Now, let's talk about how you can integrate lean principles into the very soul of an organization's culture. Making Lean a natural part of the company's ethos is a thoughtful, intentional process that must resonate with the company's vision and strategy. It requires full buy-in from leadership and active participation from every employee. To genuinely embed Lean into the corporate DNA, it's crucial to infuse these principles into everything from big-picture goals to the day-to-day grind.

Firstly, Lean principles must be embedded into the company's vision and strategy. This involves a**ligning Lean with the broader organizational goals** and ensuring that every employee understands how Lean principles contribute to these goals. Effective communication is crucial here; use town hall meetings, newsletters, and intranet portals to disseminate the Lean vision and strategy. Clear communication helps in establishing a unified direction and emphasizes the importance of Lean in achieving organizational success.

Leadership commitment is another critical factor in embedding Lean into the corporate culture. Support from top management is vital to overcoming resistance and driving Lean initiatives forward. Leaders must not only endorse Lean principles but also actively participate in Lean activities, demonstrating their commitment. Appointing Lean champions or guiding teams at various levels ensures that there are dedicated individuals responsible for maintaining the momentum of Lean initiatives and providing the necessary guidance.

Comprehensive training programs form the backbone of Lean implementation. These programs should be designed to educate all employees on Lean principles, tools, and techniques, tailored to their specific roles. Continuous learning opportunities, such as workshops, seminars, online courses, and on-the-job training, reinforce this knowledge and keep employees engaged with Lean methodologies. This ongoing education fosters a culture where Lean becomes second nature, and employees are continually looking for ways to improve efficiency.

Cross-departmental collaborations are also vital. Conducting value stream mapping sessions that involve teams from various departments helps identify inefficiencies and waste across the entire value stream.

This not only enhances process efficiency but also fosters a spirit of collaboration and teamwork. Creating cross-functional teams to tackle specific Lean projects brings together diverse perspectives and expertise, leading to innovative solutions and a more comprehensive approach to problem-solving.

To truly anchor Lean principles within an organization, establishing robust structures and systems that sustain these practices is crucial. A practical step towards this goal involves forming dedicated Lean guiding teams, such as a Lean Steering Committee and Kaizen teams, which play crucial roles in steering the Lean journey toward success.

Lean Steering Committee should be composed of senior leaders who are not only advocates of Lean principles but are also knowledgeable in its methodologies. The committee's role extends beyond administrative oversight; it involves setting clear Lean priorities, judicious allocation of resources, and diligent monitoring of the progress of Lean initiatives across the organization. This high-level engagement ensures that Lean remains aligned with the company's strategic objectives and receives the necessary support to overcome challenges.

On the operational front, *establishing Kaizen teams* dedicated to continuous improvement projects is essential. These teams, empowered to identify inefficiencies, propose solutions, and implement changes, are the engine of ongoing transformation. By organizing regular Kaizen events, organizations can maintain momentum and ensure that Lean principles transcend the realm of theory and become embedded in everyday operations.

In tandem with these teams, **a solid framework for Performance Metrics and Feedback Mechanisms** is indispensable. Developing and tracking Key Performance Indicators (KPIs) aligned with Lean objectives allows organizations to measure the effectiveness of Lean initiatives concretely. These KPIs might include metrics such as cycle time, defect rates, and customer satisfaction. Regular feedback mechanisms, through tools like surveys and suggestion boxes, complement these metrics by providing qualitative insights from both employees and customers. This dual approach ensures that Lean initiatives are grounded in real-world effectiveness and are continuously refined.

Recognition and Rewards play a key role in cultivating a Lean culture. Designing incentive programs that reward employees for their contributions to Lean initiatives can significantly boost engagement and motivation. Recognizing and celebrating successes not only reinforces the value of Lean efforts but also motivates the workforce to sustain their commitment to operational excellence.

An illustrative example of successful integration of these elements can be seen in the Hilti Corporation. Hilti's integration of Lean into its vision and strategy under the banner of operational excellence was a foundational step. Supported by strong leadership commitment from the CEO, Christoph Loos, and an extensive training framework, Hilti fostered an environment ripe for Lean principles. The establishment of a Global Lean Team ensured that Lean practices were uniformly applied across the organization, driving significant improvements in efficiency and operational performance.

Through such structured approaches, organizations can embed Lean into their corporate culture and ensure it is sustainable, adaptable, and effective in driving continuous improvement and operational excellence. This holistic implementation exemplifies how Lean can transcend being a mere methodology to become a core aspect of an organization's culture and operational strategy.

People-Centric Efficiency

Now, having explored the pillars of mindset and culture, we arrive at the third pillar of operational efficiency: people. This pillar, rooted in people-centric efficiency, underscores the pivotal role of individuals in enhancing an organization's operational efficiency. To truly understand how efficient team structures and dynamics contribute to operational success, we need to delve into three key areas: team composition, inter-team collaboration, and conflict resolution.

Team composition is fundamental to operational efficiency. Assembling teams with diverse skill sets ensures a broad range of expertise, enabling them to tackle various tasks and challenges effectively. When team members bring different perspectives and backgrounds, it leads to innovative solutions and robust problem-solving capabilities. Research supports the notion that task-relevant diversity, such as differences in expertise and functional backgrounds, positively influences team effectiveness. This diversity allows teams to approach complex tasks from multiple angles, fostering creativity and more comprehensive decision-making.

The composition of team members' personalities and cognitive abilities also plays a significant role. For instance, teams with high levels of conscientiousness tend to excel in planning and execution tasks. Moreover, cognitive diversity enhances creativity and decision-making, providing a balanced approach to achieving operational goals. By carefully selecting team members based on their skills, personality traits, and cognitive abilities, organizations can build high-performing teams that drive efficiency.

Inter-team collaboration is another crucial aspect of operational success. Effective collaboration between teams leverages combined strengths and expertise, resulting in outcomes that exceed the capabilities of individual teams. This synergy not only enhances overall operational efficiency but also promotes innovation. Cross-departmental collaboration brings together diverse ideas, experiences, and knowledge, improving the organization's problem-solving abilities. This collective approach leads to more innovative solutions to complex challenges.

Furthermore, continuous improvement is a natural outcome of effective inter-team collaboration. Teams that work well together share best practices, learn from past mistakes, and implement process enhancements. This continuous improvement cycle is essential for maintaining high levels of operational efficiency, ensuring that the organization remains agile and responsive to changing market demands.

Conflict resolution is the final piece of the puzzle. Unresolved conflicts can hinder productivity and damage team dynamics. Effective conflict resolution helps maintain a positive work environment, allowing teams to focus on their goals rather than interpersonal issues. Addressing conflicts promptly reduces stress among team members, leading to a more harmonious and efficient workplace. Lower stress levels contribute to higher job satisfaction and better overall performance.

Additionally, resolving conflicts enhances team cohesion. Promptly addressing and resolving issues builds trust and unity within the team, fostering a collaborative environment where members feel valued and supported. This sense of trust and cohesion is crucial for long-term operational efficiency, as it enables teams to work together effectively towards common goals.

The Toyota Production System (TPS) exemplifies how efficient team structures and dynamics contribute to operational efficiency. Toyota carefully selects team members based on their skills and expertise relevant to the production process, emphasizing task-relevant diversity. TPS promotes strong inter-team collaboration through regular cross-functional meetings and shared problem-solving sessions. Teams from different departments work together to identify and eliminate inefficiencies.

Toyota also promotes a culture of open communication and continuous improvement, addressing conflicts promptly and constructively. Techniques like the "5 Whys" help get to the root cause of issues and implement effective solutions. This holistic approach to team composition, collaboration, and conflict resolution has enabled Toyota to achieve exceptional operational efficiency and maintain a competitive edge in the automotive industry.

As we delve into the significance of people-centric efficiency and its role in boosting operational efficiency, it's imperative to consider how this approach aligns operations to effectively meet customer needs. This emphasis on employee engagement and empowerment enhances staff satisfaction and drives the operational agility necessary to satisfy customer demands proactively.

Empowering employees to make decisions, particularly those affecting customer satisfaction, can lead to a quicker resolution of issues and a more adaptable service model. Training and development are also crucial, equipping employees with the necessary skills and knowledge to respond effectively to customer needs. This training often covers areas such as customer service excellence, in-depth product knowledge, and advanced problem-solving techniques. Furthermore, recognition and reward programs that celebrate contributions to customer satisfaction and efficiency can significantly motivate employees, encouraging them to sustain high performance levels.

Cross-departmental collaboration plays a key role in this people-centric approach. When various departments such as sales, customer service, and operations work cohesively, the organization can offer a seamless customer experience. This holistic approach not only ensures that all customer touchpoints are synchronized but also enhances the organization's ability to innovate and solve problems more effectively. This type of collaboration brings diverse perspectives and expertise to the table, sparking innovation and fostering an environment where complex challenges are addressed more efficiently.

A compelling example of how a people-centric approach can revolutionize customer satisfaction and operational efficiency is seen in Starbucks' operational strategy. Starbucks refers to its employees as 'partners,' a nomenclature that underscores their importance to the company. These partners are provided with extensive training and development opportunities, which empower them to excel in customer service and product expertise. Such empowerment ensures that Starbucks' partners are well-prepared to meet and exceed customer expectations.

Moreover, Starbucks emphasizes strong cross-departmental collaboration. Integrating functions such as marketing, operations, and customer service enables Starbucks to deliver a consistent and personalized customer experience. The synergy between the company's loyalty program and in-store operations, for instance, facilitates efficient order processing and enriches customer interactions with personalized touches.

Starbucks also champions a culture of continuous improvement and effective conflict resolution. Partners are encouraged to handle customer complaints proficiently and to contribute feedback about operational processes. This ongoing feedback loop is vital for pinpointing improvement opportunities and implementing strategic changes that enhance both efficiency and customer satisfaction.

This people-centric approach, underpinned by strategic empowerment, comprehensive training, and cross-departmental collaboration, exemplifies how companies can transform their operations to be both customer-focused and efficient.

To boost people-centric efficiency and enable operational efficiency, organizations must focus on optimizing team composition, nurturing inter-team collaboration, and implementing effective conflict resolution strategies.

To begin with, ***optimizing team composition*** is crucial. Utilizing task analytic methods allows organizations to deconstruct tasks required for each role and pinpoint the specific skills, knowledge, and abilities necessary for effective performance. By ensuring that team members are selected based on their competencies and potential to excel in their roles, organizations can form robust teams capable of handling diverse challenges. Research networking tools play a pivotal role in identifying potential team members with the right expertise and experience, helping to locate candidates with a proven track record in similar roles or projects. Additionally, conducting behavioral interviews can assess candidates' problem-solving abilities, teamwork skills, and cultural fit. These interviews should include questions that reveal how candidates have handled similar tasks and challenges in the past, providing a clearer picture of their capabilities.

Balancing demographics within teams is another essential aspect. Ensuring that the team comprises members with diverse skill sets and backgrounds can lead to more innovative solutions and a broader range of perspectives. However, managing demographic heterogeneity carefully is crucial to avoid potential faultlines and subgroups that could hinder team cohesion. Focusing on creating a balanced mix that supports scientific productivity and effective collaboration is key. Promoting an inclusive culture where all team members feel valued and respected is vital. This can be achieved through diversity training, inclusive policies, and regular team-building activities, fostering an environment where everyone can thrive and contribute meaningfully.

Nurturing inter-team collaboration is equally important for enhancing operational efficiency. Regular cross-team meetings should be scheduled to discuss progress, share insights, and identify areas for collaboration. These meetings help break down silos and promote a unified approach to achieving organizational goals. Organizing joint problem-solving sessions where members from different teams come together to address common challenges fosters a collaborative environment and leverages the collective expertise of the organization.

Implementing shared tools and systems is essential for facilitating seamless communication and collaboration across teams. Document collaboration tools, such as PandaDoc, can help teams work together more efficiently, even in a virtual environment. Integrated communication platforms like Slack, Microsoft Teams, and Asana allow for real-time communication, document sharing, and project management. These tools ensure that efforts are coordinated, and everyone is on the same page, enhancing overall productivity and efficiency.

Moving on from how we foster team collaboration, let's dive into another vital aspect of putting people first: solving conflicts effectively. It's crucial for keeping a peaceful workplace and making sure our teams stay sharp and productive.

Effective conflict resolution begins with a proactive stance. By addressing conflicts early, organizations can prevent issues from escalating, which preserves team dynamics and productivity. Leaders should be vigilant for signs of discord, such as increased absenteeism or drops in engagement, which often precede overt conflicts.

The next step is to clarify the issues at hand. Engaging in root cause analysis involves all parties and helps uncover underlying concerns that may not be immediately apparent. Open communication is vital here, creating a safe space where everyone can express their views without fear of reprisal. This openness not only clarifies misunderstandings but also helps in forging a path toward a mutual understanding.

Mediation plays a key role when conflicts become complex. Facilitating discussions between parties in a structured setting can help deescalate tensions. It's beneficial to establish ground rules for these discussions to ensure that conversations are constructive and focused on resolution rather than blame.

Finally, following up on conflict resolution is as important as the initial intervention. Regular check-ins help ensure that agreed-upon solutions are implemented and that old tensions do not resurface. Additionally, incorporating feedback mechanisms can provide valuable insights into the effectiveness of the conflict resolution process, allowing for continuous improvement.

For instance, Zappos exemplifies this approach by empowering its employees to resolve customer issues directly, promoting cross-departmental collaboration, and maintaining an open environment for addressing conflicts. This proactive and inclusive approach enhances operational efficiency and builds a resilient organizational culture.

And that wraps up our deep dive into the core pillars of operational efficiency: mindset, culture, and people. Throughout our exploration, we've unearthed crucial insights that pave the way for refining and improving organizational operations. These aspects have laid the groundwork for what's to come.

Turning the page, we approach a dynamic and crucial topic: technology. It's a game-changer in every sector, revolutionizing operational efficiency andredefining the boundaries of what's possible. In the next part of our journey, we'll dive into how technology integrates into operational frameworks, exploring hacks that leverage tech to streamline processes and boost efficiency.

– 8 –

Leveraging Technology and Data for Operational Excellence

*"Harness technology and data to elevate
operations and achieve excellence."*

We've already unpacked the human side of operational efficiency, looking at the critical interplay of mindset, culture, and teamwork. Now, let's turn our gaze to a dynamic force reshaping every corner of our lives and businesses: technology. Bill Gates once remarked, "The advance of technology is based on making it fit in so that you don't really even notice it, so it's part of everyday life." This idea captures the essence of what modern businesses strive for—integrating technology so seamlessly that it becomes second nature, silently powering progress and innovation.

Up until now, we've skimmed the surface of what tech tools can do and how they're already shifting the business world. But there's much more to this story. This chapter dives deep into the ways technology not just supports but supercharges operational efficiency. From the precision of automation and the insights driven by artificial intelligence to the clarity brought by streamlining data processes and managing risks—technology is a transformative force.

Technology Enablers

As we delve into the essence of operational excellence, we recognize the pivotal role that advanced technologies like automation tools, artificial intelligence (AI), and enterprise resource planning (ERP) systems play in transforming business operations. These technologies are essential for enhancing efficiency, minimizing errors, and improving decision-making. However, before we proceed, it's important to emphasize a key principle: optimize the process before implementing automation.

This concept is something I have continually reiterated in my business as well. Bill Gates aptly put it, "The first rule of any technology used in a business is that automation applied to an efficient operation will magnify the efficiency. The second is that automation applied to an inefficient operation will magnify the inefficiency."

With this understanding, let's transition to discussing the various automation tools that can further enhance our operational efficiency.

Consider *automation tools*. They do more than handle mundane tasks—they empower human teams by freeing up their time to focus on more complex, strategic work. Robotic Process Automation (RPA) is a transformative technology revolutionizing operational efficiency across various industries, including manufacturing and services. By automating repetitive, rule-based tasks, RPA enables organizations to streamline processes, reduce errors, and optimize resource utilization.

In the manufacturing industry, RPA can automate tasks involved in production processes such as data entry, quality assurance, and inventory management. This automation reduces the likelihood of human errors, enhances efficiency, and shortens production times, ultimately leading to increased productivity and significant cost savings. Reports indicate that RPA can help manufacturers achieve up to 20% cost savings by automating processes like purchase order creation, invoice processing, and supply chain management.

One of the significant concerns in manufacturing is downtime, which can result in lost production, missed deadlines, and decreased revenue. RPA addresses this by continuously monitoring equipment and systems, detecting potential issues in real-time, and scheduling predictive maintenance tasks accordingly. This proactive approach helps minimize downtime and ensures smoother operations.

Quality control is crucial in manufacturing, as defective products can lead to lost revenue and damaged reputations. RPA can automate tasks such as data entry, product testing, and inspection, reducing the risk of errors and defects. This results in improved product quality, increased customer satisfaction, and higher profitability.

Supply chain management, a complex process involving multiple parties and systems, benefits significantly from RPA. By automating tasks such as order processing, inventory management, and shipment tracking, RPA enhances supply chain efficiency, reduces errors, accelerates delivery times, and optimizes inventory levels. This streamlining of the supply chain ensures that products are delivered promptly and accurately.

Manufacturing processes generate vast amounts of data, which can be challenging to manage and analyze manually. RPA automates data collection, analysis, and reporting, enabling data-driven decision-making. This capability allows manufacturers to gain insights into production processes, equipment performance, and customer behavior, leading to better-informed decisions and improved operational efficiency.

Overall, RPA's impact on the manufacturing industry is profound, driving significant improvements in efficiency, quality, and cost savings.

In the service industries, Robotic Process Automation (RPA) significantly lowers operational costs by reducing reliance on human labor, which involves training, infrastructure, and maintenance expenses. By executing tasks around the clock and adjusting operations dynamically based on demand, RPA enhances productivity and seamlessly integrates with existing systems and applications, making the entire operation more efficient.

Customer experience is also notably improved with RPA. It provides faster, more consistent service responses, reduces wait times, and minimizes human errors, allowing service agents to dedicate more time to complex and high-value interactions. Furthermore, RPA enriches customer feedback and loyalty through automated surveys and alerts following each transaction, thereby fostering a better relationship with customers.

When it comes to reporting and analytics, RPA offers enhanced visibility into service performance. It automates the collection, analysis, and presentation of critical data, including ticket volumes, resolution times, compliance with service level agreements (SLAs), customer satisfaction, and agent utilization. Automated reports and dashboards empower service managers to monitor trends, pinpoint issues, refine processes, and make data-driven decisions.

RPA proves particularly vital in industries like finance and healthcare where compliance is key. Automating compliance-related tasks such as data entry, document processing, and reporting ensures strict adherence to regulations, thereby mitigating the risk of non-compliance, potential penalties, and reputational damage.

Additionally, RPA transforms back-office operations in service industries by automating routine tasks like data entry, document processing, and report generation. This automation not only frees up staff to engage in more strategic activities but also improves overall efficiency and minimizes the error rate associated with manual processes.

While RPA brings many advantages, its successful implementation hinges on thorough planning, meticulous testing, effective governance, and robust change management. For enhanced results, organizations should consider pairing RPA with other cutting-edge technologies such as artificial intelligence and machine learning. This integration not only further boosts operational efficiency but also opens new avenues for innovation and addresses issues like labor shortages, which are prevalent in both manufacturing and service sectors.

Digital Process Automation (DPA) takes automation a step further by managing complex, full-scale business processes. Digital Process Automation (DPA) significantly enhances operational efficiency by leveraging advanced technologies to automate and optimize complex business processes. This approach integrates various systems, minimizes human intervention, and enables real-time decision-making, dramatically transforming business operations.

In the financial services industry, for instance, DPA automates the entire customer onboarding process, including KYC verification and account opening. This not only ensures compliance but also speeds up the entire procedure, enhancing customer experience by providing swift, error-free services. Similarly, in manufacturing, DPA can take over production scheduling and quality control, leading to increased production rates and improved resource utilization without the need for constant human oversight.

By automating repetitive and manual tasks, DPA significantly reduces labor costs and diminishes the likelihood of errors that lead to costly corrections. For example, automating invoice processing eliminates manual data entry and matching, reducing operational expenses while improving accuracy.

The productivity of employees is also boosted as DPA frees them from mundane tasks, allowing them to focus on more strategic activities. This shift not only increases productivity but also enhances employee satisfaction and engagement, creating a more dynamic and innovative workplace. In sectors like healthcare, DPA streamlines patient onboarding and appointment scheduling, which enhances the patient care experience and boosts overall satisfaction.

The agility and flexibility provided by DPA are crucial in today's fast-evolving business environment. It enables organizations to quickly adapt to changes in market conditions and customer demands. Automated workflows and integrated systems offer the flexibility needed to experiment with new products and services without significant risk, ensuring organizations remain competitive and responsive.

In highly regulated industries like finance and healthcare, DPA ensures compliance by automating documentation and reporting processes, which reduces the risk of non-compliance and the penalties associated with it. For instance, automating regulatory reporting and documentation management in the financial sector ensures strict adherence to legal requirements.

Supply chain management is optimized through DPA by automating tasks such as order processing, inventory management, and shipment tracking. This automation leads to faster delivery times, optimized inventory levels, and fewer operational bottlenecks. In manufacturing, integration with ERP systems through DPA provides real-time visibility into supply chain operations, further enhancing efficiency.

DPA also facilitates data-driven decision-making by providing real-time data and analytics. By automating data collection and analysis, it helps identify trends, monitor performance, and optimize processes. This capability is invaluable in industries like manufacturing where real-time data can significantly improve production efficiency and product quality.

Moreover, DPA enhances collaboration and communication across departments by automating workflows and ensuring that all stakeholders have access to the same information. This synchronization leads to more coordinated efforts and faster decision-making. In service industries, automating project management and approval processes ensures seamless team collaboration.

Finally, DPA supports scalability by enabling organizations to handle higher volumes of work efficiently without a proportional increase in resources. For example, logistics companies can use DPA to automate shipment scheduling and tracking, allowing them to manage larger volumes of shipments efficiently. This comprehensive approach streamlines operations and empowers organizations to harness the full potential of their resources and innovate continuously.

Following the transformative impact of Digital Process Automation, *IT Process Automation (ITPA)* further enhances operational efficiency by automating both routine and complex IT tasks, thus enabling IT staff to concentrate on strategic initiatives.

ITPA automates repetitive tasks such as system monitoring, software deployment, data backups, and incident management, dramatically reducing the need for manual intervention. This automation not only minimizes errors but ensures tasks are carried out consistently and efficiently. For instance, system monitoring through ITPA tools involves continuous tracking of system performance, automatically triggering alerts and corrective actions when anomalies are detected, thereby preventing downtime and ensuring smooth business operations.

The deployment of software updates and patches is also streamlined through ITPA, keeping systems secure and up-to-date without manual effort. Similarly, automated data backups ensure critical data is regularly secured, enhancing business continuity. Automated incident management further optimizes IT operations by streamlining the process from ticket creation to resolution, thereby accelerating response times and enhancing service quality.

By freeing IT staff from mundane tasks, ITPA allows them to dedicate more time to strategic projects such as digital transformation and process optimization, boosting productivity and aligning IT operations more closely with business goals. The shift to strategic initiatives fosters a more engaging and innovative working environment, directly contributing to business growth and competitiveness.

Operational costs are reduced through the minimization of manual labor and error-related corrections. For example, automating common service desk requests like password resets can yield significant cost savings, with studies suggesting that large organizations can save over $1 million annually on such support costs alone.

ITPA also plays a crucial role in enhancing compliance and security. Automated enforcement of IT policies ensures consistent application across the organization, maintaining compliance with regulatory standards and reducing the risk of penalties. Security tasks such as patch management and vulnerability scanning are handled with increased consistency and timeliness, strengthening the organization's overall security posture.

The visibility and decision-making in IT operations are significantly improved by ITPA. Real-time monitoring and automated reporting tools provide immediate insights into system status and performance, enabling IT managers to swiftly tackle issues and optimize resources. These data-driven insights help anticipate and strategically respond to operational needs, enhancing overall efficiency and performance.

Furthermore, ITPA facilitates scalability and flexibility within IT operations, crucial for organizations experiencing growth or facing changing business demands. Automated processes easily expand to handle larger workloads, and customizable tools allow for quick adaptation to new technologies or business requirements.

Lastly, ITPA improves collaboration and communication within IT teams and across departments. Automated communication tools ensure efficient information flow, aligning stakeholders and enhancing coordinated efforts across the organization. This creates a collaborative environment where strategic projects benefit from cross-functional insights and innovations.

Through these examples, we see how integrating smart technology tools into daily operations isn't just about keeping up with the times—it's about setting a foundation for sustained success and readiness for future challenges

As we continue to unpack the role of technology in operational excellence, let's dive into the transformative impact of Artificial Intelligence (AI). *Artificial Intelligence (AI) and Machine Learning (ML)* are reshaping industries by driving smarter decision-making and crafting more personalized customer interactions. These technologies extend their reach across various sectors, automating tasks, predicting outcomes, optimizing processes, and delivering unparalleled improvements in decision-making through sophisticated data analysis.

In the realm of manufacturing, AI-powered robots and algorithms transform assembly lines and inventory systems. Robots automate tasks like assembly operations and quality control inspections, ensuring products meet stringent quality standards through real-time monitoring without human intervention. This shift not only bolsters efficiency but also elevates the quality of outputs.

Service industries benefit similarly, with AI chatbots and virtual assistants managing customer interactions round the clock. These tools handle inquiries, process transactions, and support customers, enhancing satisfaction while allowing human agents to tackle more nuanced challenges. This automation streamlines operations and elevates the level of service provided to customers.

AI and ML stand out in their ability to predict outcomes. In manufacturing, predictive maintenance anticipates equipment failures, schedules timely maintenance, and avoids costly downtime. In the financial sector, these technologies analyze customer data to forecast credit risk and detect fraud, significantly enhancing risk management and personalizing customer service offerings.

The optimization of complex processes is another area where AI and ML excel. In manufacturing, AI algorithms predict demand and optimize supply chain logistics, ensuring products are produced and delivered efficiently. In healthcare, these technologies optimize patient scheduling and resource allocation, drastically reducing wait times and enhancing patient care.

Cognitive automation represents a leap forward in applying AI, merging it with robotic process automation to tackle complex tasks that require understanding and decision-making. This technology can parse through unstructured data—such as emails and social media posts— to extract actionable information. For instance, in customer feedback management, cognitive automation can analyze sentiments, categorize feedback, and initiate responses or escalate issues without human intervention. In manufacturing, AI analyzes production data to pinpoint inefficiencies and propose actionable improvements, enhancing both product quality and cost-effectiveness. In retail, AI-driven analysis of customer data personalizes marketing, optimizes pricing, and streamlines inventory management, transforming the retail experience.

Then there's Natural Language Processing (NLP). NLP allows AI systems to understand and interact in human language, making them invaluable across various customer service applications. AI-driven chatbots, for example, can manage routine customer inquiries with speed and efficiency, allowing human agents to focus on more complex issues. These chatbots are constantly learning from interactions to improve their responses, making them increasingly reliable as frontline support.

AI-powered process discovery tools identify and automate the most impactful business processes. In manufacturing, these tools pinpoint tasks like data entry and order processing for automation, driving cost savings and boosting efficiency. Service industries see similar benefits, as routine tasks like customer support and billing are automated, allowing employees to focus on strategic goals.

The rapid deployment capabilities of AI and ML significantly shorten the time to realize value from automation projects. In manufacturing, this rapid application reduces costs and improves quality more swiftly, enhancing the overall value delivered. In services, quick deployment translates to immediate improvements in customer service and operational efficiency.

Finally, AI and ML enhance security and ensure compliance across sectors. In manufacturing, AI monitors for security threats and ensures compliance through automated documentation. In financial services, AI's analysis of transaction patterns detects and prevents fraud, safeguarding both security and regulatory compliance.

These technologies are indispensable in the modern business world, catalyzing efficiency and innovation in both manufacturing and service industries.

Building on the transformative impact of Artificial Intelligence and Machine Learning, the *Internet of Things (IoT)* further revolutionizes operational efficiency across various sectors. By leveraging IoT devices and sensors, organizations gain the ability to monitor and analyze data from physical assets in real-time, opening up unprecedented opportunities for predictive maintenance, process optimization, and enhanced decision-making.

In manufacturing, IoT sensors enable predictive maintenance, continuously monitoring equipment conditions like temperature and vibration. This capability allows for timely interventions before potential issues escalate into costly failures, significantly reducing unplanned downtime and boosting overall equipment effectiveness. Similarly, in the transportation sector, IoT technology monitors critical vehicle parameters, such as tire pressure and engine temperature, optimizing maintenance schedules and enhancing fleet availability.

IoT devices also provide real-time insights into operational processes, helping organizations pinpoint inefficiencies and areas ripe for improvement. For example, in supply chain management, IoT facilitates the tracking of goods throughout their journey, optimizing inventory levels and improving delivery times while ensuring product quality through environmental monitoring.

Energy management benefits from IoT by enabling facilities to monitor and analyze energy usage, identify high consumption areas, and implement targeted energy-saving measures. This real-time data supports demand response programs and optimizes overall energy utilization, leading to cost savings and sustainability benefits.

IoT technology extends its utility to automating processes and enabling remote control of assets. In smart buildings, IoT systems automate lighting, heating, and air conditioning based on occupancy and environmental conditions, significantly reducing energy consumption while improving comfort. Industrial automation sees similar benefits, with IoT-enhanced processes boosting efficiency, consistency, and product quality through connected sensors and actuators.

The data collected from IoT devices plays a crucial role in driving strategic decision-making. In retail, for instance, real-time data on customer behavior and inventory levels helps optimize store layouts and management practices. Healthcare providers utilize IoT for remote patient monitoring, enhancing decision-making in treatment plans and resource allocation, thereby improving patient outcomes.

Moreover, IoT technology enhances workforce productivity and safety. In construction, IoT sensors track workers' locations and exposure to hazardous conditions, facilitating proactive safety measures and work schedule optimization. Field service operations benefit from IoT by improving job dispatch efficiency and providing technicians with real-time information on site conditions and equipment status.

IoT also ensures regulatory compliance and maintains quality control across industries. For example, in the food and beverage sector,

IoT sensors monitor environmental conditions during production and distribution, aiding compliance with food safety standards and reducing spoilage risks. In pharmaceuticals, IoT ensures quality control by monitoring manufacturing processes and storage conditions, helping companies adhere to strict regulatory standards.

This integration of IoT into daily operations optimizes performance, ensures compliance and improves overall business resilience, making it an indispensable asset in modern business operations.

Following the significant strides made by the Internet of Things in enhancing operational efficiency, *blockchain technology* emerges as a powerful enabler of transparency, security, and traceability across various industries. Its unique ability to provide an immutable ledger of transactions revolutionizes the way organizations operate, building trust and streamlining processes from financial services to healthcare.

Blockchain transforms the financial landscape by facilitating peer-to-peer transactions without the need for traditional banking intermediaries. This shift not only cuts transaction costs but also accelerates settlement times, exemplified by blockchain's capability to enable instant cross-border payments. In digital advertising, blockchain redefines interactions by allowing companies to engage directly with consumers, minimizing intermediaries and enhancing the relevance and efficiency of ads delivered.

The security enhancements brought by blockchain are profound. Its decentralized and cryptographic nature fortifies data against unauthorized access and alterations. In cybersecurity, blockchain could safeguard sensitive data by ensuring all modifications are consensus-verified across the network, a method that would have mitigated breaches like that experienced by Equifax. In healthcare, blockchain's application extends to secure and private sharing of patient records, enhancing both security and compliance with privacy regulations.

Blockchain's traceability features are invaluable in supply chain management. By tracking goods from origin to final destination, blockchain not only ensures product authenticity but also enhances compliance with regulatory standards. In the food industry, this capability enables quick identification and resolution of issues like contamination, while in pharmaceuticals, it prevents counterfeit drugs from infiltrating the market by meticulously tracking drug distribution.

The application of smart contracts in blockchain streamlines contract management significantly. These self-executing contracts with embedded terms automate transactions and legal agreements, reducing reliance on intermediaries and expediting processes. In the legal sector, smart contracts can transform property transactions by automating the exchange process, enhancing speed and security. Similarly, in insurance, blockchain facilitates faster and more accurate claims processing by automating data verification and claim settlements.

Moreover, blockchain optimizes supply chain operations by serving as a single source of truth for all parties involved. This unified data source reduces errors and enhances collaboration. The automotive industry, for example, benefits from blockchain in managing supply chain documentation, improving the accuracy of information and facilitating smoother operations. In retail, blockchain improves inventory management by providing real-time insights into stock levels and product movements, ensuring optimal stock availability.

Blockchain's role extends to facilitating data-driven decision-making. In the energy sector, it enables peer-to-peer energy trading, optimizing distribution and encouraging the use of renewable resources by allowing consumers to trade excess energy directly. For government services, blockchain streamlines and enhances transparency in processes such as identity management and land registration, reducing administrative costs and increasing efficiency.

Collaboration with external partners is also transformed by blockchain's transparent and secure nature. In logistics, a shared ledger ensures all parties access consistent and accurate transaction records, reducing delays and improving operational efficiency. In the food and beverage industry, blockchain fosters trust and collaboration by providing a verifiable record of products' journey from farm to table, ensuring quality and authenticity.

Blockchain technology stands out as a cornerstone for modern business operations, significantly boosting operational efficiency by ensuring transparency, security, and traceability across transactions and processes.

Continuing from the advancements introduced by blockchain technology, *cybersecurity solutions* become a cornerstone in bolstering operational efficiency within diverse organizations. These measures are crucial for protecting sensitive data, securing network infrastructures, and ensuring systems run smoothly, thereby supporting continuous operations and compliance with stringent regulations.

Effective cybersecurity strategies ensure the integrity and availability of data, which is fundamental for operational efficiency. Implementing robust encryption protocols guards sensitive data against unauthorized breaches, while regular data backups facilitate swift recovery from data losses, ensuring minimal operational downtime. For instance, automated backup solutions enable organizations to consistently save critical data to secure locations, prepared for rapid restoration in case of cyber incidents.

Moreover, Data Loss Prevention (DLP) solutions monitor and regulate data transfers, crucial for preventing unauthorized data disclosures and maintaining compliance with data protection regulations. These measures significantly mitigate the risks associated with data breaches, thereby avoiding operational disruptions.

The protection of IT systems and networks is equally critical. Utilizing firewalls and Intrusion Detection Systems (IDS) ensures that network traffic is scrutinized for suspicious activities, blocking potential threats and preventing disruptions like Distributed Denial of Service (DDoS) attacks. Endpoint security further bolsters defenses by safeguarding devices from malware, protecting the broader integrity of IT infrastructures. Regular updates and antivirus software deployments shield against known vulnerabilities, maintaining the operational readiness of all technological endpoints.

Compliance with evolving cybersecurity regulations prevents legal complications and fosters an environment of trust. Adherence to standards such as GDPR, HIPAA, and PCI DSS ensures that organizations uphold stringent security measures to protect sensitive information. Continuous monitoring and regular audits identify vulnerabilities promptly, helping maintain an ongoing state of compliance and readiness.

Incident response and recovery plans are crucial components of cybersecurity strategies. A well-prepared response plan enables organizations to manage and mitigate cyber incidents swiftly, minimizing downtime and operational impact. Disaster recovery and business continuity plans ensure that critical operations can continue unabated during and after cyber incidents, with strategies in place for rapid data recovery and system restoration.

The visibility into operational and security postures provided by cybersecurity solutions like Security Information and Event Management (SIEM) systems enhances decision-making capabilities. These systems aggregate security data from multiple sources, enabling a unified response to threats and bolstering overall security measures. Integrating threat intelligence into security operations keeps organizations ahead of potential threats, allowing them to fortify their defenses against emerging cyberattack vectors.

Finally, inspiring a culture of cybersecurity awareness through regular employee training reduces the likelihood of breaches caused by human error. Training programs that include simulated phishing exercises equip employees to recognize and avoid potential threats, crucial for maintaining a secure operational environment. Strong access control measures and privilege management ensure that access to sensitive data is strictly controlled, further securing against both external attacks and insider threats.

By implementing a comprehensive suite of security measures, organizations can enhance their resilience against cyber threats, safeguard their data, and maintain essential operations, all while complying with necessary regulatory standards.

Following the foundational role of cybersecurity in safeguarding operational integrity, the emergence of *Augmented Reality (AR) and Virtual Reality (VR) technologies* marks a significant advancement in enhancing operational efficiency across various sectors. These technologies revolutionize the way organizations train and maintain their workforce, redefining remote assistance and complex operational procedures.

In the manufacturing domain, AR and VR elevate training and skill development to new heights. Workers can engage in immersive VR simulations that replicate real manufacturing processes, allowing them to hone their skills without the risks associated with physical training. Meanwhile, AR transforms the workspace by overlaying digital instructions directly onto physical tasks, significantly reducing the learning curve for new employees and ensuring precise and efficient task execution.

Maintenance and repair operations also benefit profoundly from AR and VR technologies. AR headsets enable technicians to view schematics and manuals overlaid directly onto the equipment they are servicing, providing step-by-step guidance without diverting their attention from the task at hand. Remote assistance through AR further enhances efficiency by allowing experts to guide onsite technicians visually from anywhere in the world, drastically reducing downtime and travel costs.

Quality control processes are streamlined through the use of AR for real-time data display during inspections and VR for scenario-based training for inspectors. This dual approach not only improves the accuracy of inspections but also ensures that all products meet stringent quality standards before they reach the consumer.

VR also plays a vital role in factory layout optimization. By creating a virtual simulation of the factory floor, companies can experiment with workflow configurations and logistics to identify bottlenecks and optimize operations before implementing physical changes, thereby avoiding costly errors and enhancing productivity.

Shifting to healthcare, AR and VR are transforming medical training and patient care. Surgical training through VR offers a zero-risk environment for medical professionals to practice procedures, enhancing their skills without compromising patient safety. AR tools assist in complex surgeries by overlaying crucial information such as anatomical details and instrument navigation directly into the surgeon's field of vision, improving precision and outcomes.

Moreover, AR and VR extend their impact to enhancing patient care through innovative applications like VR-based therapy, which provides immersive environments for pain management and rehabilitation, significantly improving patient response and recovery times. AR-enhanced diagnostics and remote patient monitoring allow for more personalized and effective treatment plans, reducing the need for frequent hospital visits.

In education, AR and VR transform traditional learning environments into captivating educational experiences that significantly enhance student engagement and knowledge retention. From VR classrooms that transport students to historical sites for immersive lessons to AR applications that bring complex scientific concepts to life, these technologies foster a deeper understanding and a more hands-on approach to learning.

Retail experiences are also being revolutionized by AR and VR. Virtual showrooms and AR-based virtual try-ons provide customers with a new way to experience products before purchase, significantly enhancing customer satisfaction and reducing return rates. In store operations, VR training equips employees with the skills they need in a fully immersive setting, ensuring they are well-prepared for customer interactions.

Finally, in the construction industry, AR and VR are crucial in planning and safety training. VR allows for detailed visualization of architectural projects before physical construction commences, minimizing errors and ensuring project efficiency. AR supports on-site tasks by projecting accurate blueprints and work instructions into the physical space, guiding workers through complex procedures and ensuring adherence to design specifications.

Taking advantage of AR and VR's game-changing potential, let's look at tools for *predictive analytics and forecasting* that are turning into must-haves for boosting how things run in different organizations. These tools use historical data, advanced algorithms, and machine learning techniques to predict future trends, demand patterns, and operational needs, allowing businesses to make informed decisions and optimize processes effectively.

One of the most impactful applications of predictive analytics lies in demand forecasting and inventory optimization. By analyzing historical sales data, market trends, and customer behaviors, these tools provide accurate forecasts of future demand. This precision enables organizations to align production and inventory levels with anticipated demand, reducing the risk of overstocking or understocking. Optimizing inventory in this manner minimizes carrying costs, reduces waste, and ensures that products are available at the right time and location, significantly enhancing supply chain operations.

Predictive analytics also plays a crucial role in predictive maintenance and asset management. IoT sensors and analytics tools continuously monitor equipment performance, detecting anomalies and predicting potential failures before they occur. This proactive approach allows for timely maintenance, minimizing unplanned downtime and extending the lifespan of critical assets. By analyzing historical maintenance data and usage patterns, organizations can optimize maintenance schedules, ensuring that activities are performed at the most appropriate times to avoid operational disruptions.

In resource optimization and workforce planning, predictive analytics provides valuable insights into capacity planning and employee scheduling. By forecasting demand and operational requirements, organizations can optimize production capacity and allocate resources efficiently. These tools analyze employee data and performance metrics to forecast workforce needs, helping organizations identify potential talent gaps and develop targeted recruitment and training strategies. Optimized scheduling ensures that the right employees are in place at the right times, improving overall productivity and reducing labor costs.

Risk management and fraud detection are further enhanced by predictive analytics. By analyzing historical data and identifying patterns that indicate potential risks, organizations can develop proactive risk mitigation strategies. Predictive tools can detect anomalies in transaction data and customer behavior, identifying fraudulent activities before they escalate. Continuous monitoring ensures compliance with regulatory requirements, helping organizations avoid penalties and maintain their reputations.

In terms of customer experience and marketing optimization, predictive analytics enables personalized customer interactions and targeted marketing strategies. By segmenting customers based on their behaviors and preferences, organizations can tailor products, services, and marketing campaigns to specific segments, enhancing customer satisfaction and loyalty. Predictive tools can also identify customers at risk of churning, allowing organizations to implement retention strategies and personalized offers to retain valuable clients. Analyzing historical campaign performance and market trends helps optimize marketing efforts, improving the effectiveness and return on investment of campaigns.

As technology evolves, the capabilities of predictive analytics will continue to expand, offering organizations that embrace these tools a significant competitive advantage and operational excellence.

Building on our exploration of how predictive analysis and forecasting tools enhance operational efficiency, we now turn our attention to *Enterprise Resource Planning (ERP) systems*, which unify and streamline complex processes across an organization. This cohesion brings a new level of operational excellence, transforming traditional business practices with remarkable efficiency.

ERP systems integrate essential business functions such as finance, human resources, supply chain management, and customer relationship management into a single, comprehensive platform. This integration eliminates redundancies and enforces a standardized workflow across various departments. For instance, SAP ERP incorporates AI and analytics to deliver real-time insights, allowing businesses to swiftly adjust to changes in the marketplace.

These systems excel in automating repetitive tasks such as data entry, invoice processing, and report generation, substantially reducing human error while freeing up staff for more strategic roles. Oracle ERP Cloud, for example, utilizes AI and machine learning to enhance the efficiency of back-office operations.

Central to ERP's power is its ability to manage data centrally. By consolidating data from different departments into one unified database, ERP systems ensure that all areas of the business operate with consistent and accurate information. This centralization enhances decision-making and reduces miscommunications. Microsoft Dynamics 365 exemplifies this by integrating CRM and ERP capabilities to ensure seamless information flow and bolstered security.

Real-time business insights are another forte of ERP systems. They provide leaders with an immediate view of their business performance, enabling quick identification of issues and adjustment of strategies. For example, NetSuite's cloud-based ERP offers acute insights into financial management, e-commerce, and inventory, empowering timely and informed decisions.

Furthermore, ERP systems promote better collaboration and communication across the organization through tools that support document management and shared calendars. This helps in breaking down silos and fostering a culture of teamwork. Manufacturing ERP systems, for example, offer platforms where project progress can be monitored and collaborated on by all relevant team members, boosting both communication and productivity.

The advent of cloud-based ERP has also facilitated remote work by allowing secure access to crucial business functions from anywhere, ensuring continuity even in challenging times. This adaptability was particularly evident during the COVID-19 pandemic, where cloud ERP solutions enabled businesses to maintain operations without disruption.

In inventory management, ERP systems optimize resource utilization by maintaining ideal stock levels, thus enhancing order fulfillment rates and minimizing excess inventory or stockouts. Real-time tracking of inventory levels, combined with demand forecasts and supplier performance insights, allows businesses to manage their inventory more effectively, reducing costs and improving efficiency.

ERP systems revolutionize supply chain management by providing comprehensive visibility from procurement to delivery. This end-to-end oversight enables businesses to monitor each step of the supply chain, swiftly identifying and addressing bottlenecks, and adjusting to fluctuations in demand or disruptions in supply. For example, ERP platforms in manufacturing industries consolidate logistics, inventory control, and procurement into a cohesive framework, significantly enhancing operational agility and responsiveness.

On the financial management front, ERP systems are indispensable tools that offer robust financial analysis capabilities, including advanced budgeting, forecasting, and detailed reporting. These functionalities empower businesses to manage their finances with precision and make informed decisions based on accurate, real-time data. For instance, streamlined reporting processes facilitated by ERP systems minimize the chance of errors during data entry, expedite month-end closures, and enhance overall financial governance.

Moreover, the automation and integration capabilities of ERP systems contribute directly to cost reduction by streamlining key business operations and optimizing resource allocation. The efficiency gained through these systems often leads to substantial cost savings by reducing manual errors and improving the speed and accuracy of business operations. Businesses leverage ERP functionalities to quickly retrieve essential information for stakeholders, thus enhancing customer service, employee satisfaction, and operational pace.

To illustrate the transformative impact of ERP systems, consider the examples of Amazon and Starbucks. Amazon utilizes SAP ERP to harness advanced analytics powered by AI and machine learning. This integration allows Amazon to gain real-time insights into critical aspects of its operations, from financial management to supply chain dynamics, ensuring that it can adapt quickly to changes in the marketplace. Similarly, Starbucks employs Oracle ERP, a cloud-based solution that automates numerous back-office and daily operations. Oracle's comprehensive analytics enhance Starbucks's ability to monitor its efficiency and cost-effectiveness across global operations.

These examples underscore the profound influence ERP systems have on modern business operations, streamlining complex processes and equipping companies with the tools necessary for thriving in today's dynamic market environments.

The Data Advantage

Data has long been a cornerstone in business operations, but the explosion of technological advancements has catapulted it into a critical role for operational efficiency. As we transition from discussing enterprise systems, let's explore how leveraging big data and analytics can fundamentally reshape decision-making processes, refine forecasting, and lead to sharper strategic insights.

Big data is revolutionizing the way companies make decisions. By sifting through massive datasets from diverse sources—like social media interactions, detailed sales transactions, and sensor outputs—businesses can uncover hidden patterns and trends. For example, Netflix leverages such data to understand viewer preferences deeply, shaping their original content to better match audience tastes. The result includes hits like "House of Cards" that capture viewers' imaginations and set new standards for data-driven content creation.

The real-time capabilities of big data are equally transformative. With technologies that process information instantaneously, companies can now react to market changes with unprecedented speed. This agility is crucial in areas such as supply chain management, where understanding real-time dynamics can help companies quickly resolve disruptions and maintain smooth operations.

Furthermore, big data enhances risk management. It allows companies to anticipate and mitigate potential issues before they escalate. Through predictive analytics, for instance, businesses can predict machinery failures before they happen, schedule timely maintenance, and avoid costly downtime.

Leveraging the vast pools of data that modern technologies afford, organizations are taking their forecasting capabilities to new heights. Enhanced forecasting not only sharpens accuracy in predicting future demand but also transforms how businesses manage inventory, satisfy customers, and fine-tune their production strategies.

Take demand forecasting, for instance. Through the application of machine learning algorithms, businesses can sift through historical sales data, alongside market trends and other external variables, to predict future demand with remarkable precision. This precision facilitates more strategic inventory management, which can drastically reduce costs—manufacturers, for example, can cut inventory levels by up to 30% by syncing production closely with anticipated demand.

The concept of demand sensing further illustrates the agility big data brings to operational strategies. By capturing and analyzing real-time data, companies can immediately spot changes in demand. Retailers, for instance, can monitor social media to catch emerging trends as they develop, allowing them to adjust inventory dynamically. This real-time responsiveness not only meets customer expectations more effectively but also prevents the pitfalls of overstocking.

Moreover, big data empowers businesses to segment their customer base with unprecedented granularity. With detailed analysis, companies can tailor their marketing and product offerings to distinct customer segments, enhancing engagement and boosting conversion rates. Coca-Cola, for instance, leverages image recognition and data analytics to craft highly targeted ads that resonate deeply with diverse consumer groups, significantly lifting engagement levels.

Strategic decision-making also gains a robust layer of intelligence from big data. By continuously monitoring a spectrum of variables—from market trends and consumer behavior to internal operations and competitor moves—businesses can swiftly identify new opportunities and mitigate potential threats. Google, for example, analyzes employee data to optimize its workplace practices, ensuring high levels of staff retention and satisfaction.

Big data also revolutionizes the validation of business assumptions. By rigorously analyzing data from various feedback channels, companies can test their hypotheses in real-world scenarios, ensuring that their strategies are theoretically sound and practically viable.

Lastly, the strategic allocation of resources becomes more scientific with big data. By dissecting operational data, businesses can pinpoint inefficiencies, streamline processes, and channel resources into the most productive areas. Predictive maintenance technologies in manufacturing are a prime example, boosting system uptime and slashing costs by preemptively identifying and addressing potential equipment failures.

Building on the foundations laid by data-driven decision-making, organizations are now pushing the boundaries of operational efficiency. This transformation is marked by more streamlined processes, enriched customer experiences, and an adaptive approach to real-time operational adjustments.

Streamlining processes through big data analytics goes beyond merely collecting vast amounts of information; it involves a meticulous analysis to pinpoint inefficiencies and devise strategies to eliminate them. For example, in supply chain management, analytics can reveal critical bottlenecks that once addressed, significantly speed up operations and reduce costs. This optimization might involve reconfiguring logistics or automating certain steps in the production line to enhance overall efficiency.

The impact of big data extends to enhancing customer experiences. By thoroughly analyzing customer interactions and feedback, companies can uncover deep insights into customer preferences and behavior. This understanding allows businesses to tailor their services and products more precisely, boosting customer satisfaction and fostering loyalty. Personalized marketing, informed by individual customer data, not only increases the effectiveness of promotional efforts but also enhances customer engagement.

Moreover, the capability of real-time monitoring and adjustments stands out as a game-changer in operational management. Big data analytics enables companies to monitor their operations continuously and make adjustments on the fly. This agility is crucial in manufacturing environments where real-time data on production lines can pinpoint inefficiencies immediately, allowing for swift corrective actions that minimize downtime and maximize productivity.

Building on the transformative power of real-time monitoring and process optimization, another crucial aspect where big data and analytics enhance operational efficiency is through refined data governance and the leveraging of advanced analytics tools.

Streamlining Data Governance forms the backbone of efficient data management, ensuring that the information fueling decision-making processes is of the highest quality and integrity. By establishing rigorous data governance frameworks, organizations can enforce standards and protocols that ensure data accuracy, consistency, and security. Tools like Alteryx, Trifacta, or Talend revolutionize data management by automating the cleansing and preparation phases. These advanced technologies not only safeguard data quality but also liberate data professionals to dedicate more time to strategic analysis rather than routine data maintenance.

Leveraging Advanced Analytics Tools dramatically amplifies the potential to unlock operational efficiencies. Machine learning algorithms dive deep into data to reveal patterns and predict trends that escape conventional analysis, such as anticipating equipment failures or optimizing inventory levels based on predicted market demands. For example, using predictive analytics to schedule maintenance prevents costly downtime and extends the lifecycle of equipment. Similarly, visualization tools such as Tableau and Power BI transform raw data into intuitive, actionable visual dashboards. These dashboards provide leaders with at-a-glance insights into key performance metrics, enabling them to make informed decisions swiftly and adjust strategies in real time.

Let's delve deeper into how big data facilitates optimal resource allocation and real-time adjustments, crucially enhancing customer experiences.

Optimizing Resource Allocation with dynamic strategies enables organizations to adapt resource distribution based on immediate needs and conditions. In manufacturing environments, big data analytics refines the deployment of labor and machinery to match fluctuating production demands. This dynamic resource allocation minimizes idle times and maximizes output, ensuring resources are utilized effectively and efficiently. Additionally, through employee performance analytics, organizations gain the ability to pinpoint underperformance, tailoring training and development efforts to boost productivity and better employ human capital.

Moreover, *integrating the Internet of Things (IoT) and sensors* provides a granular view of operational metrics. Sensors on equipment stream data that not only track performance but also forecast maintenance needs, thus preventing downtime and optimizing workflow.

By implementing these specific and in-depth efficiency hacks, organizations can leverage big data and analytics to enhance their operational efficiency, reduce costs, and improve overall performance.

Streamlining Workflows: From Chaos to Clarity

Building on the role of big data in enhancing decision-making and operational efficiency, it's clear that technology also plays a crucial role in simplifying complex processes. The challenge often lies not just in adopting new technologies but in rethinking how every workflow and process is structured and executed.

Simplifying Complex Operational Processes begins with clarity—seeing every step and its purpose. *Process mapping and visualization* are foundational. By employing tools like Lucidchart or Microsoft Visio, organizations can create visual representations of workflows. These maps aren't just diagrams; they are revelations, highlighting redundancies and inefficiencies that, once seen, can't be unseen. For instance, a detailed flowchart might reveal that several steps in a procurement process are redundant, offering clear opportunities for consolidation.

Lean methodologies further enhance this process simplification. Principles such as value stream mapping and the 5S system do more than cut fat—they refine the workflow to ensure it's delivering maximum value with minimum waste. Consider Toyota, a pioneer in applying lean techniques, which has dramatically cut costs and improved output by consistently applying these principles to remove unnecessary steps and optimize production flows.

Standardization and documentation solidify these gains. When processes are standardized, variability is reduced, making outcomes more predictable and errors fewer. Documenting these processes in detailed standard operating procedures ensures that every team member, regardless of location or shift, can execute tasks with the same level of efficiency and precision. A classic example is McDonald's, where standardization across global outlets ensures that customers receive the same quality and service, whether they're in New York or Tokyo.

Eliminating Redundant Steps involves continuous vigilance. *Regular process audits* are essential for maintaining operational efficiency. These audits scrutinize each part of a process to ensure it's necessary and adds value. Sometimes what was once vital may no longer be relevant due to changes in technology or business practices.

Engaging employees—the people who live with these processes day in and day out—provides invaluable insights. Their firsthand experience can highlight unnecessary steps that may be invisible at the managerial level. Workshops or brainstorming sessions with employees can be gold mines for practical ideas on streamlining operations.

Building on streamlined processes, it's crucial to dive deeper into the technologies reshaping how organizations operate. The introduction of sophisticated workflow automation tools and comprehensive systems integration is a leap towards radically enhancing productivity and eliminating age-old bottlenecks.

Consider the power of tools like ServiceNow, Salesforce, and Microsoft Teams. These software products are transformation agents that automate the mundane, like invoice approvals, turning hours of manual work into a few clicks, drastically reducing errors, and freeing up time for more strategic tasks.

Then there's the integration of systems, a critical step for seamless operations. When CRM meets ERP, for instance, it's not just data that merges but a whole new level of interdepartmental synergy. This union ensures real-time access to unified customer insights, significantly boosting the responsiveness of customer service operations.

Artificial Intelligence (AI) and Machine Learning take this a step further by injecting predictive power into daily operations. These technologies are the new decision-makers, capable of analyzing vast datasets to forecast needs and identify patterns, from predicting equipment failures to optimizing maintenance schedules, thus avoiding downtime before it even threatens productivity.

And let's not overlook the flexibility brought by mobile and cloud solutions. These technologies stretch the workspace beyond traditional boundaries, enabling teams to perform from anywhere. Cloud-based project management tools like Asana or Trello enhance collaboration, ensuring that every team member, no matter where they are, stays on the same page, driving projects forward with efficiency and agility.

Integrating these technological advancements means transforming workflows to make them efficient, resilient and adaptable, ready to meet the challenges of a rapidly evolving business environment.

Risk Mitigation

As we move towards the concluding themes of our exploration of operational excellence, let's delve into a critical aspect where technology truly proves its mettle: risk management. Technology steps up significantly here, transforming how we identify, assess, and mitigate risks to ensure sustained operational efficiency.

Automated risk identification tools have revolutionized the risk management process. These tools can scan project documentation, stakeholder communications, and external data sources to spot potential risks and emerging trends. For example, sentiment analysis techniques can sift through emails and social media to detect early signs of dissatisfaction or potential project threats, providing a level of comprehensiveness and accuracy that manual methods can't match.

Risk modeling and simulation tools further enhance our capabilities. By creating various scenarios and assessing their potential impacts, these tools enable organizations to perform quantitative risk analysis and sensitivity analysis. This data-driven approach allows risk managers to make informed decisions and prioritize responses effectively. Imagine using a simulation tool to foresee the effects of a supply chain disruption and proactively developing contingency plans.

Enhancing cybersecurity measures is another crucial aspect where technology plays a vital role. Implementing advanced measures like encryption, multi-factor authentication, and continuous monitoring can significantly mitigate the risk of cyberattacks. For instance, encryption ensures that even if unauthorized access occurs, the data remains unreadable. Continuous monitoring tools like Splunk can detect and respond to threats in real-time, preventing data breaches and minimizing potential damage.

Integrating risk management systems with other business applications ensures seamless data flow and comprehensive oversight. When a risk management platform is integrated with ERP and CRM systems, it provides a unified view of risks across the organization. This integration reduces data silos, ensuring all departments have access to real-time risk information and enabling more effective mitigation strategies.

Regular risk assessments using advanced tools keep organizations ahead of potential threats. These tools evaluate the likelihood and impact of identified risks, allowing for prioritization of mitigation efforts. For instance, quarterly assessments using risk evaluation software can help identify new risks and ensure existing strategies are still effective.

Utilizing cloud-based solutions for risk management provides flexibility and scalability, adapting to changing risk landscapes. Cloud solutions enable real-time collaboration and access to risk management tools from anywhere, ensuring that risk mitigation efforts are unhindered by geographical constraints. For example, a cloud-based project management tool can facilitate real-time updates and collaboration on risk mitigation plans, making it easier to manage risks on a global scale.

This proactive approach ensures sustained operational efficiency and resilience, keeping the organization prepared and agile in the face of evolving challenges.

As we wrap up our exploration of how technology shapes and sharpens operational efficiency, it's clear that the journey doesn't end here. The tools and strategies we've discussed are essential gears in the ever-turning wheel of business operations. The way technology integrates into our daily operations subtly shifts the ground under our feet, making agility and foresight more achievable than ever.

But what happens next? As we continue to delve into this terrain of operational efficiency, how do we ensure that these efficiencies are a sustained advantage? The answer lies ahead, where we will delve into sustaining operational efficiency over the long haul.

CHAPTER

– 9 –

Sustainability and Long-Term Efficiency

"Sustainable practices ensure long-term efficiency and a resilient future."

We've journeyed through the myriad techniques and hacks for establishing and boosting operational efficiency within your organization. As we approach the final stretch of this roadmap, we find ourselves on the cusp of excellence and efficiency, gazing into the horizon of continuous improvement. This is a vital moment to embrace a crucial reminder: operational efficiency isn't a milestone to pass but a relentless pursuit to sustain. The journey you've taken on with this guide equips you with the essential knowledge to continuously enhance efficiency and ensure growth.

Winston Churchill once perfectly encapsulated this ethos, stating, "Continuous effort – not strength or intelligence – is the key to unlocking our potential." His words resonate deeply as we delve into the core of sustaining operational efficiency in any organization.

The Importance of Sustaining Operational Efficiency

Firstly, lets look at the importance of sustaining operational efficiency in an organisation. When you prioritize efficiency, you unlock a cascade of benefits that ripple through every part of your business, driving growth and fostering resilience.

One of the most immediate and tangible benefits of maintaining operational efficiency is the significant cost savings. By cutting down on waste, optimizing how you use your resources, and streamlining processes, your organization can save substantial amounts of money. These savings aren't just about trimming the fat—they can be reinvested in growth initiatives, enhancing employee skills, or increasing shareholder returns. Imagine reallocating funds previously lost to inefficiencies towards new product development or expanding your market reach. This kind of strategic reinvestment fuels innovation and sets the stage for sustainable growth.

Beyond cost savings, operational efficiency boosts productivity and throughput. Efficient operations mean you can do more with what you have, producing higher outputs without increasing input costs. This capability allows you to meet customer demands more swiftly, adapt to market changes with agility, and stay a step ahead of your competitors. For instance, an optimized production line not only speeds up manufacturing but also improves the consistency of output, ensuring that your customers receive their orders on time, every time.

Quality and consistency are vital to building a strong brand reputation. Efficient operations ensure that your products or services meet high standards consistently. By minimizing errors and defects, you not only reduce the costs associated with rework and returns but also build trust with your customers. Consistent quality enhances customer satisfaction and loyalty, which are critical for long-term success. When your customers know they can rely on you, they're more likely to return and recommend your business to others.

In a world where market conditions, customer preferences, and regulatory landscapes can shift rapidly, agility and adaptability are more important than ever. Efficient operations give your organization the flexibility to pivot quickly in response to new opportunities or threats. This agility ensures that you're not just reacting to changes but anticipating them, allowing you to stay ahead of the curve. For example, if a new regulation impacts your industry, having streamlined processes means you can adjust your operations swiftly to maintain compliance and avoid disruptions.

Operational efficiency also empowers better decision-making through data-driven insights. Access to accurate, timely, and relevant data enables you to make informed decisions that optimize performance and resource allocation. This approach moves you away from guesswork and towards a culture where decisions are backed by solid evidence. For instance, using data analytics to track performance metrics can highlight bottlenecks in your processes, providing a clear path to improvement and innovation.

Furthermore, maintaining operational efficiency fosters a proactive rather than reactive business environment. By continuously monitoring and refining your processes, you can identify potential issues before they become significant problems. This proactive stance not only enhances operational stability but also positions your organization to seize new opportunities as they arise.

Sustaining operational efficiency is not just about maintaining the status quo; it's about driving your organization towards continuous improvement and long-term success.

The Sustainable Operational Efficiency Framework

Having explored the vital importance of sustaining operational efficiency, I trust you now grasp the intricacies involved. It's time to dive deeper into practical solutions with a framework I've developed over years of experience—the Sustainable Operational Efficiency Framework. This set of hacks is a transformative journey through the essential practices that fortify and maintain efficiency within any organization. Let's walk through each component, step by step.

First and foremost, fostering a culture that embraces *continuous improvement* is crucial. This environment encourages every employee, from the ground floor to executive levels, to actively seek out inefficiencies and propose innovative solutions. Imagine a workplace where regular feedback sessions and training programs are the norms, not the exceptions, and where employees are recognized and rewarded for their ideas. This approach doesn't just solve problems—it builds a more engaged and proactive workforce.

Next, the ***regular review and assessment*** of business processes are fundamental. Through thorough process audits, your organization can shine a light on existing inefficiencies, pinpoint bottlenecks, and discover areas ripe for enhancement. This proactive audit strategy goes beyond mere oversight; it's about actively refining your operations to reduce waste, cut costs, and better allocate resources. Think of it as a regular health check-up for your business operations, ensuring everything runs smoothly and efficiently.

Efficient communication is the backbone of any successful operation. Implementing a centralized communication platform can drastically reduce email overload, cut down on misunderstandings, and keep everyone from interns to CEOs informed and aligned. This step simplifies interactions within your team and ensures that critical information is shared promptly and clearly. Picture a work environment free from the chaos of missed emails and unclear instructions, where everyone moves in harmony towards common goals.

Automation is a key player in enhancing operational efficiency. By identifying and automating repetitive, time-consuming tasks, your organization can significantly reduce the manual labor required. This minimizes human error and frees up your team to focus on more strategic and rewarding tasks. Envision your team redirecting their efforts from mundane tasks to areas that truly benefit from human insight and creativity, boosting overall productivity and job satisfaction.

Next, ***a solid performance management system*** is essential. Such a system should track key performance indicators (KPIs), set clear and achievable goals, and provide regular, constructive feedback to everyone in the organization. It's about turning performance management into a dialogue—a dynamic part of your operational strategy that supports growth and excellence.

As we delve deeper into the Sustainable Operational Efficiency Framework, ***optimizing your supply chain*** becomes a crucial step. By implementing a sophisticated supply chain management system, you can streamline procurement, inventory management, and logistics. This approach reduces costs, improves delivery times and enhances customer satisfaction. Imagine a system that automatically adjusts inventory levels based on real-time sales data, or one that chooses the most efficient delivery routes. Such innovations refine operational workflows and ensure that your supply chain is responsive to market changes and consumer demands, sustaining long-term efficiency.

Incorporating lean principles into your operations is essential for maintaining efficiency. Lean management focuses on creating value by eliminating waste and improving process flow. This methodology helps reduce variability in operations, enhancing consistency and reliability. By continually identifying and removing waste, your organization becomes more agile and better equipped to deliver high-quality products and services efficiently, sustaining operational excellence over time.

Data analytics is a powerhouse for sustaining operational efficiency by providing deep insights into every aspect of your business. Leveraging big data allows you to uncover hidden patterns, predict market trends, and understand customer behavior. This knowledge enables strategic, informed decisions that keep you ahead of the curve. For example, predictive analytics can forecast future demand spikes, enabling proactive inventory management that avoids both excess stock and stockouts, ensuring ongoing efficiency.

A solid knowledge management system is crucial for maintaining operational efficiency. Such a system captures and stores valuable knowledge, making it accessible across the organization. This prevents knowledge loss and fosters innovation. Imagine a platform where employees can easily access expertise and insights from across the organization, dramatically speeding up problem-solving and reducing the learning curve for new employees. This continual access to knowledge supports sustained efficiency and growth.

Regular employee feedback sessions are vital for sustaining operational efficiency. These sessions provide a platform for employees to voice concerns, suggest improvements, and share insights. This continuous loop of feedback and action helps identify and address issues promptly and aids in coaching and developing talent. Ensuring your team meets and exceeds their potential is key to maintaining long-term operational efficiency.

Implementing a change management process is essential for sustaining efficiency during transitions. Change is inevitable, whether from internal adjustments or external pressures. A structured change management process helps your organization adapt smoothly, with minimal disruption. It provides a clear roadmap for implementing change, ensuring all stakeholders are aligned and that the organization can quickly return to full operational capacity. This structured approach to change ensures that efficiency is maintained even during periods of transformation.

As we explore the path to sustainable operational efficiency, embedding *thoughtful systems and programs* becomes essential for shaping our organization's future. These steps are about laying the groundwork for continuous evolution and responsiveness to the ever-changing business landscape.

Starting with a customer feedback system, consider this a direct line to the core of our market. Gathering and analyzing feedback provides us with insights into what our customers really want and how effectively we're meeting their needs. This ongoing dialogue with our customers helps make our organization adaptable, enabling us to innovate in ways that keep us competitive and responsive.

For *talent development*, envision creating an environment where our brightest minds feel continuously challenged and supported. This approach goes beyond retaining top talent—it empowers them to drive innovation within our operations. A robust talent development program prepares us for today's challenges and paves the way for new solutions that will define our future success.

Risk management is often viewed as a defensive strategy, but it's fundamentally about ensuring smooth operations and safeguarding our company's assets. By proactively identifying, assessing, and mitigating risks, we can prevent disruptions and maintain continuity. This kind of proactive planning is crucial for maintaining operational flow and ensuring that efficiency is constant, even in the face of unexpected challenges.

Optimizing travel and expense management offers another strategic advantage. Streamlining these processes reduces costs and administrative burdens, enhancing overall efficiency. Adopting automated solutions and policies that ensure compliance and fiscal responsibility can lead to significant savings and a more focused operational team, free from the distractions of logistical inefficiencies.

Lastly, *implementing a sustainability program* aligns with corporate social responsibility and offers strategic benefits that impact our bottom line. Reducing our environmental footprint can also lead to savings in energy consumption, waste management, and raw materials. More than that, it positions us as a forward-thinking leader in sustainability, increasingly important to consumers and potential business partners alike.

This comprehensive approach secures our journey towards operational efficiency as both progressive and enduring. It ensures that our organization is efficient today and continues to lead in operational efficiency as it adapts to future challenges and opportunities.

Methodologies for Sustaining Operational Efficieny

As we continue to build on the foundational strategies laid out in our Sustainable Operational Efficiency Framework, it's essential to dive deeper into the specific methodologies that ensure the longevity and sustainability of these practices. Each methodology we adopt is tailored to enhance efficiency and to embed it deeply within the organization, ensuring it becomes part of our ongoing operational ethos.

Total Quality Management (TQM) serves as a cornerstone for sustained operational efficiency. This comprehensive approach is rooted in a relentless focus on customer satisfaction, recognizing that true quality extends beyond the products or services to every interaction within the organization. TQM involves a systematic look at what customers expect and then aligning your processes to meet these needs consistently. It integrates the entire organization, from the ground up, encouraging continuous improvement and data-backed decision-making. With TQM, quality becomes a pervasive culture, ensuring that every process is refined and that excellence becomes a habit.

Benchmarking extends our vision beyond the internal workings of our organization to glean insights from the wider industry landscape. By regularly measuring our operations against those of the industry leaders and innovators, we identify not just gaps but opportunities for significant improvement. Benchmarking is a robust, ongoing process that drives us to maintain a competitive edge and adapt best practices that refine our operational strategies. This method keeps us perpetually on the path to improvement, ensuring we are always aligned with, or ahead of, market standards.

The Balanced Scorecard technique broadens our approach to measuring success. It introduces a multi-faceted view of performance, spanning financial results, customer satisfaction, internal process efficiency, and innovation and learning. This strategic tool links performance metrics with overarching organizational goals, facilitating a balanced approach to assessing and sustaining efficiency. It ensures that as we strive for financial health, we also prioritize customer loyalty, process integrity, and continuous learning and growth among our staff.

Business Process Reengineering (BPR) involves the radical redesign of core business processes to achieve dramatic improvements. It's about not being afraid to rethink how we work to significantly boost productivity and efficiency. BPR looks at the essence of our business processes and strips them down to rebuild more streamlined, cost-effective, and efficient operations. This methodology requires bold thinking and a willingness to implement deep structural changes that can lead to substantial improvements in performance and efficiency.

Total Productive Maintenance (TPM) emphasizes proactive and preventative maintenance to avoid breakdowns and ensure smooth operations. It involves every employee in the maintenance process, from operators to managers, fostering an environment where everyone is responsible for the optimal performance of equipment and processes. TPM reduces downtime and increases productivity by maintaining equipment at its peak condition, thus extending its lifecycle and enhancing its reliability.

Alongside these methodologies, tools such as *Business Intelligence (BI) and Process Mining* empower us to sustain these efficiencies. BI tools allow us to make informed, data-driven decisions by visualizing key performance metrics and predicting future trends. Process Mining provides a microscopic view of our processes, identifying inefficiencies and confirming the conformity to intended workflows, which is crucial for continuous improvement.

As we explore the methodologies for sustaining operational efficiency, we must consider the essential practice of ensuring **consistent operational excellence.** This approach is vital for several compelling reasons.

Enhanced customer satisfaction is one of the foremost benefits of operational excellence. When every interaction with your customers is efficient and consistent, it builds a foundation of trust and loyalty. Delivering products or services on time, with fewer errors and delays, and maintaining consistent quality leads to positive customer experiences. This satisfaction fosters repeat business, enhances your brand image, and is crucial for long-term operational efficiency.

Improved product quality is another critical outcome of operational excellence. By embedding stringent quality control measures throughout the production process, organizations can reduce errors, ensure consistency, and maintain high standards. Meeting or surpassing customer expectations builds brand trust and credibility, which reduces the need for rework and returns, further sustaining operational efficiency.

Operational excellence also significantly boosts productivity. Streamlining workflows, cutting waste, and refining processes lead to higher output with fewer resources. This increased efficiency translates directly into a stronger bottom line, making it a cornerstone for sustained operational efficiency.

Creating a culture of continuous improvement is another key advantage. Encouraging employees to identify inefficiencies and suggest improvements cultivates innovation and problem-solving. This adaptability enhances processes and performance, ensuring that the organization remains agile and can sustain operational efficiency over time.

Reducing operational costs is a direct benefit of focusing on eliminating waste and optimizing processes. Lower costs mean more resources can be allocated effectively, whether investing in new technologies or improving other business areas. This careful resource management is vital for sustaining operational efficiency.

Operational excellence also supports agility and resilience, enabling organizations to respond swiftly to internal challenges or changes in market demand. This adaptability maintains continuity and stability, allowing businesses to seize new opportunities and address challenges without significant disruptions.

Achieving operational excellence gives organizations a competitive advantage, allowing them to outperform peers in key metrics such as cost, speed, and service quality. This edge attracts a broader customer base, helps maintain market leadership, and secures strategic partnerships and investments, all of which are essential for sustaining operational efficiency.

Better risk management is another significant benefit. Operational excellence involves proactive problem-solving and continuous process monitoring, helping identify and mitigate risks early. Effective risk management ensures smooth operations without unexpected disruptions, contributing to sustained operational efficiency.

Finally, operational excellence often leads to higher employee engagement and retention. When employees are empowered to contribute to process improvements and see the impact of their efforts, job satisfaction increases. This engagement reduces turnover costs and ensures the organization retains valuable talent, which is critical for maintaining operational efficiency.

Incorporating sustainability into every aspect of our operations also plays a vital role. By adopting energy-efficient technologies and waste reduction strategies, we cut costs and align our operations with broader environmental and social governance criteria, enhancing our reputation and compliance.

As we discuss the importance of ensuring consistent operational excellence in sustaining operational efficiency, I would like to delve into a specific methodology that embodies this principle: *the DMAIC methodology*. This structured, data-driven approach to problem-solving and process improvement plays a crucial role in maintaining and enhancing operational excellence.

The DMAIC methodology starts with the Define phase, where the focus is on clearly identifying the problem, setting the scope, and outlining goals and customer requirements. Utilizing tools such as project charters and SIPOC diagrams helps create a clear understanding of the problem at hand. This stage also involves ensuring that the problem definition aligns with the organization's strategic goals and objectives, setting a solid foundation for the subsequent phases.

Moving into the Measure phase, it's essential to establish a baseline by measuring the current state of the process. This involves collecting data on process performance and identifying key metrics. A robust data collection methodology is developed to evaluate success and gather accurate current state data, providing a clear picture of where improvements are needed.

In the Analyze phase, the focus shifts to identifying and validating the root causes of process variations and poor performance. Techniques such as root cause analysis and failure mode and effects analysis (FMEA) are employed to delve deep into the issues. Developing a precise problem statement and validating the root causes ensures that improvement efforts are targeted at the right issues, paving the way for effective solutions.

The Improve phase is where solutions are developed and implemented to address the identified root causes. This involves generating and evaluating solution ideas, conducting pilot tests, and refining solutions based on feedback. Effective implementation requires rolling out the changes and communicating them to all stakeholders, ensuring smooth adoption and buy-in from the team.

Finally, the Control phase focuses on sustaining the improvements over time. Monitoring the process using control plans, statistical process control (SPC), and mistake-proofing (poka-yoke) ensures that the gains achieved are maintained. Documenting the new processes and providing training ensures that everyone follows the improved procedures consistently, embedding the changes into the organizational essence.

This framework addresses immediate problems and builds a culture of continuous improvement, ensuring long-term operational efficiency.

By integrating these methodologies into our daily operations, we ensure that the operational efficiency we have achieved is sustainable, adaptable, and deeply ingrained in our organizational culture.

Future-Proofing for Sustained Operational Efficiency

Shifting from discussing methodologies for maintaining efficiency, let's explore how to shield our operations from future uncertainties. Future-proofing is about being agile enough to ride the waves of change.

To tackle upcoming challenges and market shifts, fostering organizational adaptive capacity is key. This means building an environment where flexibility and learning are part of the everyday ethos. Imagine an organization where teams are connected through hierarchy and a web of diverse interactions that encourage innovation and resilience. Here, redundancy isn't about excess but about having a cushion—extra bandwidth in systems and processes that allow you to experiment and respond without risking the core operations. Additionally, embracing loose coupling gives different parts of the organization the freedom to adjust quickly without waiting for a central directive. This flexibility can be crucial when quick pivots are necessary, allowing units to respond effectively to immediate needs without entangling others.

Digital transformation is the next frontier in future-proofing our operations. This involves adopting new technologies and fundamentally reshaping how we operate to stay relevant and competitive. By leveraging cloud computing, we minimize our reliance on physical infrastructures, which reduces costs and increases our agility. Cloud platforms can scale with demand, providing the elasticity needed to handle market fluctuations smoothly.

Incorporating AI and machine learning into our systems transforms our approach to market challenges. These technologies enhance our ability to predict trends, automate routine tasks, and make informed decisions swiftly, ensuring that our operations are not just efficient but also intelligently responsive to changing conditions. As discussed in the previous chapter, the Internet of Things (IoT) provides unprecedented control and visibility over our operations, equipping us with real-time data to optimize and anticipate business needs.

Continuing to refine our strategies for future-proofing operations, it's imperative to emphasize strategic flexibility. This means cultivating the ability to swiftly adapt and reconfigure resources and processes in response to shifting market conditions. A crucial tool in this effort is scenario planning, which involves crafting multiple detailed scenarios that help predict various future states. This preparation enables your organization to have ready responses, mitigating potential disruptions. Moreover, creating modular systems that can easily be adjusted or scaled as circumstances dictate enhances this flexibility. Equally important is agile decision-making—establishing processes that allow your organization to make quick decisions that are responsive to new information and rapidly changing conditions.

In today's business climate, integrating sustainability and Environmental, Social, and Governance (ESG) factors into your operations isn't just ethically sound—it's strategically smart. This integration enhances long-term resilience and operational efficiency. By managing a sustainable supply chain, for instance, you ensure that your suppliers uphold environmentally sound practices, reducing your overall environmental impact. Investing in energy-efficient technologies cuts costs and diminishes your ecological footprint, aligning your operational practices with broader global sustainability goals. Additionally, engaging in Corporate Social Responsibility (CSR) initiatives can significantly bolster your organization's reputation and strengthen relationships with stakeholders, creating a solid foundation of trust and cooperation.

Investing in continuous learning and development is also crucial for maintaining a workforce capable of navigating change. By regularly updating training programs to reflect the latest technological advancements and industry best practices, you ensure that your team remains at the cutting edge. Facilitating a culture of knowledge sharing allows valuable insights and methods to circulate freely across your organization, fostering an environment where innovation thrives. Leadership development should also focus on nurturing skills that support adaptability, innovation, and strategic foresight. Leaders equipped with these competencies can guide their teams through complex changes and challenges, ensuring that your organization survives and thrives in the face of future uncertainties.

As we continue our journey towards a resilient future, the intelligent use of data becomes increasingly important. Moving toward a resilient future, mastering the art of data utilization becomes crucial. It's about transforming raw data into actionable insights that drive efficiency. Advanced data analytics help us understand our operational performance and spotlight areas ripe for improvement. Implementing real-time monitoring allows us to adjust our strategies swiftly, ensuring smooth and responsive operations. Predictive maintenance uses data patterns to anticipate and prevent breakdowns, optimizing our workflow and preventing disruptions before they start.

Embracing a customer-centric approach, we recognize that innovation hinges on necessity and relevance. By integrating customer feedback into our development process, we ensure that our products and services evolve in meaningful ways that resonate with users. Personalization, powered by data, enhances customer experiences, boosting satisfaction and fostering loyalty. Agile product development practices enable us to adapt our offerings quickly based on real-time feedback, keeping us aligned with market demands and customer needs.

In managing risks and building resilience, we proactively protect our operations from potential threats. Regular risk assessments prepare us to navigate various scenarios, while comprehensive business continuity plans guarantee that our operations continue smoothly under adverse conditions. Our crisis management teams are equipped and ready to act, safeguarding our operations and the people behind them.

Strategic partnerships and collaboration expand our capabilities and fuel innovation. Encouraging collaboration across different departments allows us to harness diverse perspectives and skills, sparking groundbreaking ideas. Our external partnerships, from suppliers to research institutions, are not merely alliances; they are vital extensions of our capabilities, driving mutual growth and innovation.

Finally, fostering a culture that values flexibility and embraces innovation secures our long-term relevance and resilience. In this environment, we welcome change and view it as an opportunity for advancement. We promote an innovation mindset where taking calculated risks is encouraged, propelling us to explore new frontiers. Employee engagement is crucial—it's a reflection of our organizational health and directly influences our operational efficiency and output quality.

This holistic approach ensures that we maintain efficiency today and continue to innovate, making us well-prepared to meet the future challenges of a dynamic business environment. Each strategy is a step toward mastering the evolving challenges and seizing opportunities in an ever-changing market.

This brings us to the end of our core discussion on operational efficiency. As we stand at the final part of our roadmap, what lies ahead is a horizon brimming with possibilities. As you prepare to take your first steps into this world of operational excellence, I encourage you to glance back at these pages one last time. Let this be a farewell that fills you with a sense of completeness and confidence.

Every strategy we've explored, every insight shared, is a tool for your journey. Embrace them with an open mind and a determined spirit.

Synthesis and The Path Forward

We have traversed a path leading to operational excellence throughout the pages of this book. As we reach the end of this journey, it is essential to reflect on the path we have traveled. Steve Jobs once said, *"You can't connect the dots looking forward; you can only connect them looking backwards."* This sentiment perfectly sums up the essence of our exploration. By looking back, we gain clarity and understanding of the steps that have brought us to this point.

In this book, we have traversed a roadmap designed to guide you through three critical stages of strengthening operational excellence. We began with *Part I: Operational Efficiency for Modern Business Leaders*. Here, we laid the foundation of efficiency by defining operational efficiency in today's business environment. We emphasized the importance of process optimization, resource allocation, and leveraging technology. The discussions highlighted how global changes, such as the COVID-19 pandemic and rapid technological advancements, have reshaped the need for operational efficiency, making it more relevant and urgent than ever.

Next, we delved into assessing operational health. This involved understanding what constitutes operational health through industry-specific benchmarks and standards. We explored innovative diagnostic tools like predictive analytics and AI-driven diagnostics, which provide real-time insights into your operations. These tools are not just about identifying problems but also about predicting and preventing them, thus ensuring that your operations run smoothly and efficiently.

Building a foundation for excellence was the next step. We discussed the necessary structural changes required to support and enhance operational efficiency. This included restructuring teams, integrating advanced technology, and building a resilient operational framework. Leadership's role in this transformation was emphasized, showcasing how strategic decision-making and clear efficiency goals can drive an organization toward sustained excellence. The integration of advanced technologies, such as AI and machine learning, was highlighted as a crucial factor in supporting these structural changes and enhancing overall operational efficiency.

By focusing on these core strategies in Part I, we established a strong foundation for operational excellence. Continuing our journey, we ventured into *Part 2: Operational Agility: Adapting to a Rapidly Changing World.* Here, we defined operational agility, distinguishing it from general business agility. We emphasized the critical role of responsiveness, flexibility, and resilience in day-to-day operations. In an era where change is constant, the ability to swiftly adapt and respond to new circumstances is paramount. Operational agility ensures that organizations can pivot effectively, maintaining performance and service quality despite the shifting market.

We then explored the implementation of agile principles. Introducing methodologies like Scrum and Kanban, we delved into how these frameworks facilitate agile operations. By focusing on creating agile teams, we highlighted the importance of structuring teams to be cross-functional and self-organizing, enabling them to react quickly to changes and continuously improve processes. Measuring agility using specific key performance indicators (KPIs) provided a tangible way to assess progress and effectiveness. These KPIs, such as cycle time, team velocity, and customer satisfaction, offer clear metrics to track the benefits of agile practices.

Transforming operations through agility was brought to life through detailed case studies. These real-world examples demonstrated the profound impact of adopting agile operations. We analyzed the before and after effects, showcasing the tangible benefits and challenges overcome. Organizations that embraced agility saw improved efficiency, faster time-to-market, and enhanced customer satisfaction. The case studies provided practical insights into how companies navigated their transitions, the obstacles they faced, and the innovative solutions they implemented to achieve their goals.

By focusing on operational agility, we equipped you with the tools and knowledge to make your organization more responsive and resilient. These strategies ensure that your business can survive and thrive amidst uncertainty, turning potential challenges into opportunities for growth and innovation.

In Part 3 of our journey, titled *Efficiency Hacks: Transforming Operations in Today's World,* we dove deep into the crucial interplay between mindset, culture, and people that underpins operational efficiency. It's about fostering an environment where efficiency permeates every aspect of the organization. We discussed how instilling an efficiency mindset, embracing Lean principles, and nurturing a people-centric approach can transform how teams operate and engage with their work.

We also explored the transformative impact of technology and data in driving operational excellence. By harnessing advanced tools like AI, ERP systems, and big data analytics, we can streamline workflows and make more informed decisions, allowing us to stay ahead in a rapidly evolving marketplace.

Sustainability also played a key role in our discussions, highlighting how integrating sustainable practices not only benefits the environment but also bolsters long-term operational success. By measuring and maintaining improvements in efficiency, organizations can contribute positively to the broader community while enhancing their own operational viability.

These strategies are part of a broader framework designed to sustain operational excellence. This framework is built on three pillars: operational efficiency, agility, and continuous improvement, each supporting and reinforcing the others to create a robust, adaptable organization.

Operational efficiency lays the foundation, ensuring that every process is optimized, resources are utilized effectively, and technology is leveraged to its full potential. On this solid base, operational agility allows the organization to quickly adapt to changes and challenges, ensuring that efficiencies gained are not just temporary but built to last.

Lastly, the drive for operational excellence is continuous. It demands regular evaluation and refinement, keeping the organization at the cutting edge of industry standards and practices. This involves pushing boundaries and continuously seeking ways to do better.

As we wrap up our exploration together, I want to encourage you to take these strategies and make them your own. Dive into the principles of operational efficiency, agility, and excellence we've discussed. Start small if you need to, implement these strategies, track your progress, and stay committed to excellence. This involves transforming how you operate on a day-to-day basis.

The path to operational excellence is ongoing. It doesn't end with the last page of this book. It's a continuous commitment to adapting, improving, and being ready to meet whatever challenges come your way. With the right approach and tools, this journey will enhance your current operations and prepare you to thrive amidst the inevitable changes of the business world.

Think of this as more than a business strategy; see it as a mindset that permeates every level of your organization. Let these ideas inspire you to innovate and push the boundaries of what you believe is possible in your field.

So, as you move forward from here, let the insights from our time together guide you. Use them to drive your organization toward a future where excellence is part of your core identity. Here's to your journey ahead—may it be as rewarding as it is successful.

Appendix

Worksheet 1

Assessing and Enhancing Operational Efficiency

Section 1: Understanding Operational Efficiency

Define Operational Efficiency in Your Context

Task: Develop a detailed, contextual definition of operational efficiency that aligns with your organization's goals and industry standards.

Action: Create a list of key elements that define operational efficiency within your organization, such as process optimization, effective resource allocation, and strategic technology utilization. Ensure these elements are measurable and aligned with overarching business objectives.

Impact of Global Changes

Task: Reflect on recent global events and their impacts on your operations.

Action: Analyze and document how these events have reshaped your strategy and approach to operational efficiency. Consider changes in consumer behavior, supply chain disruptions, or shifts in regulatory environments, and outline strategic adjustments made in response.

Section 2: Assessing Operational Health

Benchmarking

Task: Identify and document industry-specific benchmarks that relate to operational health.

Action: Conduct a detailed comparison of your current operational performance against these benchmarks. Utilize a SWOT analysis to provide a structured evaluation of strengths, weaknesses, opportunities, and threats related to your operational health.

SWOT Analysis for Operational Insights

Task: Perform a SWOT analysis focusing on your operational processes.

Action: Detail strengths, weaknesses, opportunities, and threats associated with your operations. Use this analysis to identify critical areas for improvement and potential strategic advantages.

Pinpointing Inefficiencies

Task: Employ process mining and workflow analysis to uncover areas of inefficiency.

Action: Collect and analyze feedback from both employees and customers to identify operational pain points. Use this data to target process enhancements and increase overall operational responsiveness and efficiency.

Section 3: Building a Foundation for Operational Excellence

Structural Changes

Task: Examine your organizational structure for necessary changes to enhance operational efficiency.

Action: Develop a plan to either centralize or decentralize functions, restructure teams, or integrate advanced technology to streamline operations and enhance productivity.

Leadership Role

Task: Define the optimal leadership styles and strategies that foster and support operational efficiency.

Action: Craft a comprehensive leadership strategy that emphasizes operational efficiency, including setting clear goals, aligning incentives, and fostering a culture of accountability and efficiency across all levels of the organization.

Continuous Improvement

Task: Implement and institutionalize continuous improvement cycles (Plan-Do-Check-Act).

Action: Establish a schedule for regular assessments to review and enhance operational processes continuously. Ensure each cycle yields actionable insights that lead to tangible improvements.

Worksheet 2

Implementing and Sustaining Operational Agility

Section 1: Defining Operational Agility

Characteristics of Agile Operations

Task: Enumerate the essential characteristics of agile operations such as responsiveness, flexibility, and resilience.

Action: Develop strategies to incorporate these characteristics into your daily operations, ensuring they align with your organizational goals and enhance your ability to adapt quickly to changes.

Agility and Technology

Task: Identify technologies that bolster operational agility, such as cloud computing, artificial intelligence (AI), and the Internet of Things (IoT).

Action: Create a comprehensive integration plan for these technologies. Detail how each technology can be implemented to streamline operations, enhance data-driven decision-making, or improve customer interactions.

Section 2: Implementing Agile Principles

Agile Methodologies

Task: Select an agile methodology that aligns with your operational needs (e.g., Scrum, Kanban).

Action: Outline the process for adapting this methodology to fit your operational processes, including timelines, expected challenges, and resource allocation.

Creating Agile Teams

Task: Design team structures that maximize agility—consider cross-functional teams that can rapidly adapt and respond to change.

Action: Clearly define roles, responsibilities, and the interaction flow within these agile teams to ensure everyone understands their part in driving agility.

Measuring Agility

Task: Establish key performance indicators (KPIs) and metrics that effectively measure agility, such as cycle time and lead time.

Action: Set up systems to regularly track, analyze, and report these metrics to gauge the success of agile practices and identify areas for improvement.

Section 3: Transforming Operations Through Agility

Case Studies and Lessons Learned

Task: Analyze several case studies of companies that have successfully implemented operational agility.

Action: Summarize the key lessons from these case studies and discuss how they can be adapted to fit your organization's specific context.

Sustainable Agility

Task: Formulate strategies to ensure the sustainability of agility practices over the long term, focusing on continuous learning and adaptation.

Action: Consider potential future trends in operational agility and develop proactive plans to embrace these trends, keeping your operations at the cutting edge.

Worksheet 3

Implementing Efficiency Hacks

Section 1: Cultivating Efficiency: Mindset, Culture, and People

Efficiency Mindset

Task: Define what an efficiency mindset means specifically for your organization, emphasizing a systematic approach to continuous improvement.

Action: Develop comprehensive strategies to cultivate this mindset across all levels of the organization. This could include leadership training, employee workshops, and reward systems that recognize efficiency improvements.

Lean Culture

Task: Outline the essential elements of Lean principles relevant to your organization, such as Kaizen (continuous improvement), Just-in-Time (minimizing waste by receiving goods only as they are needed), and Jidoka (automating with a human touch).

Action: Plan concrete steps to integrate these Lean principles into your corporate culture. This might involve setting up regular training sessions, creating cross-departmental teams to implement lean projects, and tracking progress with specific metrics.

People-Centric Efficiency

Task: Evaluate how your team structures and dynamics currently contribute to or detract from operational success.

Action: Develop strategies to enhance team efficiency, such as optimizing team composition, encouraging open communication, and empowering employees to innovate and take the initiative in identifying efficiency improvements.

Technology Enablers

Task: Identify specific technologies that can drive operational excellence within your organization, including automation tools, AI, and ERP systems.

Action: Create a detailed plan for integrating these technologies into your operations. This plan should consider current technological infrastructure, required upgrades, and potential barriers to implementation.

Data-Driven Decision Making

Task: Develop a strategy for harnessing big data and analytics to enhance decision-making processes.

Action: Identify critical data points and establish a system for ongoing data collection and analysis. Set up dashboards and reporting tools that make data easily accessible and actionable.

Streamlining Workflows

Task: Map your current workflows and identify potential areas for simplification and enhancement.

Action: Implement technology solutions to eliminate redundant steps and automate routine tasks, creating more streamlined and efficient workflows.

Section 3: Sustainability and Long-Term Efficiency

Sustainability and Efficiency

Task: Explore how integrating sustainability practices can enhance operational efficiency within your organization.

Action: Develop strategies to measure the impact of sustainability initiatives on operational efficiency and to sustain these improvements over time. Consider energy efficiency upgrades, waste reduction programs, and sustainable sourcing practices.

Long-Term Planning

Task: Prepare for the future by planning how to future-proof your operations against anticipated challenges and market changes.

Action: Focus on building agility and the capacity for rapid adaptation. Outline specific actions such as scenario planning, investing in scalable technologies, and developing a flexible workforce.

Operational Health Checklist for Business Leaders

This checklist is designed to help business leaders systematically ensure the operational health of their organization, fostering an environment of efficiency, resilience, and continuous improvement.

Financial Health

- Review and update the financial reporting framework to ensure accurate periodic reporting and cash flow forecasts.
- Analyze financial ratios to assess liquidity, profitability, and operational efficiency.
- Evaluate budgeting and forecasting processes for alignment with strategic business goals.

Sales and Marketing

- Assess sales performance to identify improvement areas in sales strategies.
- Review the effectiveness of current marketing campaigns.
- Evaluate customer acquisition and retention strategies for consistency and growth potential.

Operations and Processes

- Streamline operational workflows to eliminate bottlenecks and inefficiencies.
- Assess inventory management and supply chain processes for effectiveness.
- Evaluate customer service procedures and integrate feedback mechanisms.

Human Resources

- Identify skills gaps and training needs within teams.
- Review employee satisfaction and engagement levels.
- Evaluate the effectiveness of recruitment and onboarding processes.

Technology and Systems

- Evaluate the current technology infrastructure and software applications.
- Ensure robust IT security measures and data protection protocols are in place.

- Identify opportunities for automation and process streamlining through technology.

Risk Management

- Review and ensure insurance coverage aligns with business risks.
- Assess the effectiveness of business continuity and disaster recovery plans.
- Identify and address potential legal or regulatory compliance issues.

Strategic Planning

- Regularly review progress towards long-term business goals.
- Evaluate the competitive landscape and market trends.
- Adjust strategic planning processes as needed to stay current.

Compliance and Legal Requirements

- Verify adherence to industry regulations and contractual agreements.
- Implement and maintain internal controls for fraud prevention and asset safeguarding.
- Conduct regular audits to ensure compliance with standards.

Customer Focus

- Implement effective and responsive customer service operations.
- Use customer feedback to drive product and service improvements.
- Ensure high-quality standards are maintained in all customer interactions.

Innovation and Adaptability

- Encourage continuous learning and adaptability within the organization.
- Invest in research and development to stay ahead of market trends.
- Implement agile methodologies to enhance organizational responsiveness.

Monitoring and Review

- Schedule and conduct regular reviews of all operational processes.
- Use data analytics to gain insights into operational performance.
- Adjust strategies based on audit findings and performance data.

This checklist provides a structured approach to monitor and enhance various aspects of operational health, ensuring their organization remains efficient, resilient, and competitive in today's dynamic business environment.

Operational Excellence Checklist for Business Leaders

This checklist is designed to help business leaders systematically build and sustain operational excellence, ensuring their organizations are efficient, resilient, and competitive.

Strategic Alignment

- **Define Vision and Mission:**

  Clearly articulate and communicate the organization's vision and mission.

  Ensure strategic objectives are aligned with the vision and mission.

- **Set Strategic Goals:**

  Establish SMART (Specific, Measurable, Achievable, Relevant, Time-bound) goals.

  Cascade these goals throughout the organization to ensure alignment at all levels.

Process Management

- **Optimize Key Processes:**

  Define key processes using SIPOC (Suppliers, Inputs, Process, Outputs, Customers) models.

  Standardize processes while maintaining flexibility for specific situations.

- **Implement Continuous Improvement:**

  Adopt methodologies such as Lean, Six Sigma, and Kaizen for ongoing process improvement.

  Conduct regular process audits and root cause analyses to identify and eliminate inefficiencies.

Performance Management

- **Develop Performance Metrics:**

  Establish balanced scorecards with KPIs aligned with strategic goals.

Use dashboards to visualize performance metrics and track progress in real-time.

- **Conduct Regular Reviews:**

Schedule regular performance review meetings to assess progress and address gaps.

Ensure meetings result in actionable decisions and clearly defined next steps.

Technology Integration

- **Leverage Advanced Technologies:**

Integrate automation tools, AI, and ERP systems to streamline operations.

Utilize data analytics for informed decision-making and predictive insights.

- **Ensure Robust IT Infrastructure:**

Implement cloud computing and IoT for real-time monitoring and operational agility.

Maintain cybersecurity measures to protect data integrity and ensure operational continuity.

Employee Engagement and Development

- **Foster a Culture of Continuous Learning:**

Provide ongoing training and development opportunities for employees.

Encourage a growth mindset and innovation through regular workshops and seminars.

- **Empower Employees:**

Promote autonomy and decision-making at all levels of the organization.

Recognize and reward contributions to operational excellence.

Sustainability and Efficiency

- **Measure and Sustain Efficiency Gains:**

   Use tools and methodologies to track the impact of efficiency improvements.

   Regularly review and adjust strategies to maintain long-term efficiency.

By following this checklist, business leaders can systematically achieve and sustain operational excellence, ensuring their organizations are prepared to thrive.

Additional Resources for Reference

Books

- "The Lean Six Sigma Pocket Toolbook" by Michael L. George, John Maxey, David Rowlands, and Mark Price

- "The Goal" by Eliyahu M. Goldratt and Jeff Cox

- "Lean Thinking" by James P. Womack and Daniel T. Jones

- "The Toyota Way" by Jeffrey K. Liker

- "Six Sigma for Managers" by Greg Brue and Robert G. Launsby

- "Hoshin Kanri for the Lean Enterprise" by Thomas L. Jackson

- A detailed guide on strategic planning and policy deployment using Hoshin Kanri to align organizational goals with operational activities.

- "The Lean Enterprise Memory Jogger" by Richard L. Macinnes

Articles and Websites

Lean Partner: Visit *www.LeanPG.com* for bespoke training and consultancy services tailored to driving business transformation and operational excellence across various industries. Lean Partner offers a range of solutions from automation to certifications, aimed at enhancing operational capabilities in organizations, from Fortune 500 companies to government agencies.

Productive.io: What Is Operational Efficiency? Examples & Strategies - A comprehensive guide on operational efficiency, including examples and strategies to enhance business performance.

Enate Blog: Improving Operational Efficiency in Healthcare - Insights into improving operational efficiency in healthcare, detailing challenges and expert advice.

Authors' Profile

MANICKAVASAGAM PALANIANDY

Founder | CEO at Lean Partner and MyRAG360
Transformation Expert | Principal Consultant |
Coach Speaker | Author| Master Black Belt

With over 27 years of experience in diverse industries such as manufacturing, oil, gas, energy, and banking, Manickavasagam Palaniandy stands as a preeminent expert in business transformation and operational excellence. His career began in manufacturing engineering, where he honed his skills in Lean Six Sigma, earning credentials from the prestigious Six Sigma Academy in the Netherlands. Manickavasagam has held key roles in multinational corporations, where he distinguished himself as a global leader and consultant.

In 2013, driven by his commitment to excellence, Manickavasagam founded Lean Partner. This boutique consulting firm specializes in business transformation and operational excellence, providing training and consultancy services that span automation, certifications, and more. Today, Lean Partner supports over 200 clients, including Fortune 500 companies and government bodies, with tools and methods designed to enable world-class operational capabilities.

In his book, "The Efficiency Edge: Transforming Business Operations for Future Success", Manickavasagam draws on his extensive background to offer leaders actionable insights for transforming their organizations. He focuses on inspiring resilience, enhancing efficiency, and maintaining competitiveness in the evolving business world.

ABOUT LEAN PARTNER

Our Vision

To be Asean's leading training and consultancy firm that enables organizations to transform their processes, enhance cost efficiency, user friendliness, customer intimacy & superior responsiveness.

Our Mission

SMART PROCESSES, SMART RESULTS

We design smart processes through customized consultation services based on specific consumer needs for maximum business results.

VALUE TRANSFER

We provide knowledge and guidance through highly skilled professional trainers to achieve positive transformation with tangible results.

GIVING BACK TO SOCIETY

We implement diverse and far-reaching Corporate Social Responsibility (CSR) initiatives that benefit the marketplace, the community at large and the environment as well as our own employees' well-being.

www.LeanPG.com